# Eunuchs in Politics
# or
# Politics in Eunuchs?

## About the Author

**Ayub Khan** is Professor of Sociology at Maharani Laxmi Bai Government College of Excellence, Gwalior (M.P.). He has been a fellow associate of the Indian Institute of Advanced Study, Shimla for three years. His research interests include marginalized groups, culture and communication, health and society, population, etc. He is the published author of "*Female Adolescent Workers: Faceless and Fateless*". He has also completed projects sponsored by the ICSSR and the UGC apart from contributing articles to various national and international journals.

*This book is*
*dedicated to my wife*
**Sumita**
*who has been an inspiration throughout the process of completing this book.*
*Also to my children*
**Azan & Ayaan**
*who give me a deep satisfaction of being a father.*

# Eunuchs in Politics or Politics in Eunuchs?

Ayub Khan

CONCEPT PUBLISHING COMPANY PVT. LTD.
NEW DELHI-110059

ISBN-13 : 978-93-5125-163-7

First Published 2015

*Published and Printed by*

Concept Since 1974

**Concept Publishing Company Pvt. Ltd.**
A/15-16, Commercial Block, Mohan Garden
New Delhi-110059 (India)
*T*: 25351460, 25351794, *F*: 091-11-25357109
E: publishing@conceptpub.com, W: www.conceptpub.com
**Editorial Office:** H-13, Bali Nagar, New Delhi-110 015, India.

Cataloging in Publication Data--Courtesy: D.K. Agencies (P) Ltd. <docinfo@dkagencies.com>

**Khan, Ayub, author.**
Eunuchs in politics or politics in eunuchs? / Ayub Khan.
pages cm
Includes bibliographical references (pages ) and index.
ISBN 9789351251637

1. Eunuchs--India--Madhya Pradesh. 2. Eunuchs--Political activity--India--Madhya Pradesh. 3. Politicians--India--Madhya Pradesh. 4. Madhya Pradesh (India)--Politics and government. I. Title.

DDC 306.7609543 23

extremely thankful to him. My special thanks to Dr. K.D. Prasad, Regional Director, IGNOU, New Delhi for his appreciation and assistance in statistical analysis of data.

The study tours conducted to collect data for my research meant travelling the length and breadth of Madhya Pradesh. I also acknowledge the contributions of The National Library, Kolkata and The Indian Institute of Advanced Study, Shimla from where I gathered most of the literature. In preparing this book I have had invaluable assistance of Mr. Evangel Athial, who has done most of the reading and correction. I have also had a number of helpful suggestions from him. I am also grateful to Mr. Ashok Kumar Mittal and Concept Publishing Company (P) Ltd., New Delhi for bringing out this book in a short time. The author also wishes to gratefully acknowledge the services of Mr. Deepak Mittal in the preparation of printed material in time.

Finally, I would like to thank all the eunuch politicians as well as the entire eunuch community who became part of this work, served as key informants, respondents and gracious hosts. I would also like to thank all those people who positively or negatively motivated me to accomplish my work.

This book will stimulate and encourage many people to understand the efforts of some eunuchs to merge into the mainstream through politics rather than considering their sufferings as challenge to their manhood and womanhood.

I sincerely hope that the findings of this research will be considered as scattered seeds, which will grow in the near future.

**Ayub Khan**

# Prelude

For quite some time the author has been studying eunuchs very closely and was trying to unveil their shrouded identity. Traditionally, they are allotted some space in the Indian society, which one feels is constricting. They sing and dance at births, weddings and other auspicious occasions and are compensated in cash and kind. But, with the old order breaking down, people follow these customs less and less. The eunuchs are having no option but to adapt to other ways for livelihood.

Many names have emerged in various professions but in Madhya Pradesh some promising names emanated and captured the headlines of the news especially in politics like Shabnam Mausi, Kamala Jaan, Kamala Bua, Heera Bai, etc. Interestingly in order to make better rapport with the local people (voters) they established personal relationship by adding *'bua', mausi'* as suffixes to their names and assured the society that they too are part of it. Most of the eunuchs are involved in local politics contesting as independent candidates. Continuous wins in various elections created chaos in the state politics of Madhya Pradesh. The success stories challenged the political entity of the mainstream politics. By hook or crook attempts were made to let them down in public, humiliate on the basis of their gender crisis and traditional occupation. Though they were proved to be novices in the field of politics by the old aces, the traditional *guru-chela* relationship was giving way to new relations of friendship in the political sphere.

However, in the past eunuchs had enjoyed power and had become generals, treasurers, chamberlains and diplomats. Many of them proved to be trustworthy and rose to prominence within the imperial courts.

After a long interlude, eunuchs are again accessing into the politics. Fed up with the corruption and polluted politics people are giving chance to the eunuchs, hoping their sterility will work in modern context. In turn eunuchs are using their sterility or their inability to generate heirs as their weapon in Indian polity. The few success stories of the community in Madhya Pradesh, became inspiration for other members of the community. This changing political behaviour instigated the author to develop this study.

Though the study of elections has been generally seen as a concern of the political scientists, due to my prolonged association with eunuch community, I could not overlook their behavioural changes. Through this study I have attempted to explore and analyse the political behaviour of eunuchs of Madhya Pradesh. I am really thankful to University Grants Commission, Central Regional Office, Bhopal for the financial aid and support for the completion of this study. However, the present book emerged from the aforementioned project as well as my other related researches.

A book that represents various perspectives of eunuchs requires the support and contributions of many agencies and people. I am intellectually indebted and would like to express my deep gratitude to Prof. Satish K. Sharma of H.P. University, Shimla who provided constant encouragement and guidance during different phases of this study. I am thankful to honorable Justice Jitendra Kumar Maheshwari, High Court of M.P., Bench at Indore for providing me the legal eye. I would also like to thankfully acknowledge Mr. Virender Singh, the then 1st Additional District Judge, Katni (M.P.) for quoting my studies in the case of *Kamala Jaan Vs. Alka Jain & others.*

I was looking for a cartoonist who could grasp the essence of these narratives and draw a picture of each to enhance its value. I am happy to have found one in Irfan Khan who has very kindly provided several illustrations for the book. I am

# List of Tables

# Contents

## List of Coloured Pictures

# One
# Introduction

The eunuchs have suddenly begun attracting attention of the mass-media. Many films, books and television documentaries have converged on the eunuchs. Their strange world of bizarre faces, betel chewing red mouths, effeminate figures, ill-fitting women's costumes, loud clapping, bawdy gestures and postures and many other aspects of their life styles make the stories spicy and spine-tingling. The eunuchs, for the normally gendered, are the archetypal 'others'. Are they born that way or are they victims of castration? The eunuchs themselves do not offer any help in resolving this puzzle. They refuel it at every encounter by flaunting their ambiguous sexuality through embarrassingly overt mannerisms. Their unabashed strip-tease is sure to make people shrink away.

Perhaps they have a stake in continuing to be the sexual enigma, because the folk myths surrounding them give them a brand identity—the third sex—which helps them in earning their livelihood. But the society treats them as social inferiors, marginalised, stigmatised and persecuted. This neglect is largely due to the intellectual, social and morally defined strictures of sexual dimorphism or they are considered enigmatic individuals who are often talked about but rarely understood.

Doomed by sexual deformity and shunned by society, the eunuchs are struggling to carve a niche for themselves in the vast Indian subcontinent, some eunuchs have chosen different missions like modelling, social work, politics, etc. Eunuchs have started re-inventing themselves. Till 1986, eunuchs in India were even deprived of the fundamental right to vote. The urge to be part of the mainstream of society and to have the right to vote in their own chosen identity, had been growing in the community for quite sometime.[1] The movement raised by the community led to the Election Commission's direction to its officials in 1993 to include eunuchs on the electoral rolls (*The Telegraph*, Calcutta, 12 March 2005). The Election Commission's direction had two immediate results. First, it was just like flood-gates opened for 'political eunuchs'. They sparkled as demonstrably honest politicians in mofussil towns of Punjab, Haryana, Rajasthan, Madhya Pradesh, etc., secondly, the victory of handful eunuchs in various elections is proof that eunuchs who were long ostracised as freaks, are starting to merge into the society to gain mainstream respect.

They converted their setback of sexual handicappedness into strength and bachelorhood as their asset. In 1999, when Kamala Jaan filed her nomination to the post of Mayor for the city of Katni, people of Madhya Pradesh acceded the slogan—

*'Kamal Nahin Kamala Chahiye*
*Panja Nahin Chhakka Chahiye'*

Kamala Jaan struck headlines when she became the first eunuch in India to be elected to the post of Mayor. Soon, Kamala Jaan started running the city of Katni with an iron hand. 'Subjugated by a eunuch'—this very feeling tingled many politicians/people. They started posing questions and cast aspersion on her triumph. It was said that Indian voters were frustrated or disgusted with corrupt politicians that is why they voted for eunuchs to snub the established political parties. How a shunned person could succeed was really difficult to accept? By and by few disappointed people instigated adversarial and resistance politics. Finally, the confusion over the gender tag for her has been ragged. Ultimately, Kamala Jaan's candidature had been reprimanded as illegal and disqualified her from the mayoral post. The law identified her as male against her wish, as in some older documents she was listed as Kamaluddin. Illiterate Kamala Jaan failed to prove her candidature, but her setback could not hold back the stunning march of the 'third gender' into electoral politics.

Enticed by the eminence of Kamala Jaan in society many more eunuchs intruded the 'politics of recognition' and didn't repeat the mistake. Following Kamala Jaan, Shabnam Mausi was elected as M.L.A. from Sohagpur constituency of Shehdol in the year 2000, Rani Jaan from Sehore, Heera Bai from Jabalpur and Gulshan from Bina were elected as councillors. Whereas, Meena Bai of Sehora became Chairperson of the Municipal Committee, Shanti Bai of village *Dhamanka,* tehsil *Dabra,* District Gwalior became member of Zila Parishad as a Congress candidate. Besides these, there are many more eunuchs who fought in the ballot field but lost the battle. Their aspiration and behaviour shows that eunuchs in Madhya Pradesh specifically are no more dormant. In 2001, they formed a '*Hijra Mahasangh*' to fight the local and general elections in different parts of the country (*The Times of India,* New Delhi, 20 June 2001). In October 2003, eunuchs of M.P. formed a '*Jeeti Jitai Party*' (already won party) and decided to contest state elections on 71 seats under the party banner (though the party has not yet been registered).

The changed behaviour of eunuchs in democratic India attracted the media spotlight and highlighted as an unusual event, which in fact is not. History is evident that many eunuchs had political functions in different parts of India during different reigns. But after Mughals their glaze became dwindled with time. Not only people forgot about those eunuchs but also the eunuchs do not have reminiscences about those eunuch politicians. However, average eunuchs had always remained more or less in the same condition—gloomy, humiliated and ostracized.

The success stories of Santosh of Bhuchho Mandi, a town in Bhatinda district (Punjab), Nagina of Hanumangarh (Rajasthan), Basanti Sharma of Sriganganagar (Rajasthan) and Shobha Nehru of Hissar (Haryana) were unknown in Madhya Pradesh until the victory of Kamala Jaan. A new social identity of Kamala Jaan stimulated the eunuchs in the state. Since then their behaviour seems to be changing. The profession of entertaining guests at weddings, births and asking for money on other social celebrations too became merely the means to earn their living. Politics crave the new arena in their lives.

I have been working on eunuchs for more than a decade and have observed the change in the issues of their conversation. Their prolonged gossip converges on politics, either in criticizing the participation of eunuchs into politics or appreciating the attempt. Anyway I realised the fact that eunuch community have started dreaming politics. This aspect of the behaviour plays an important role in forming political attributes and inculcating democratic values among the eunuchs and bears a lasting effect on their personality.

This study is an attempt to evaluate factors relevant to eunuchs' participation in the political realm of M.P. In other words, the present study seeks to throw some light on the inevitable questions like—what made eunuchs politicians? Is the identity crisis or need of recognition driving them towards politics? Are they becoming politically active due to the popularity of certain eunuchs? Is their participation in politics an indication of departure from the traditional role or is their victory in elections, considered a step towards social acceptance for the community? A sincere attempt has been made to resolve such conundrums pragmatically in the present study.

## Objectives of the Study

The present study is undertaken with a broad objective—to analyse the political behaviour of the eunuchs of Madhya Pradesh.

In this study 'political behaviour' is used in a restricted and technical sense to cover studies designed to produce scientifically verifiable propositions about their conduct in political situations. Here, political behaviour includes political consciousness, political participation and political value orientation. The attempt was also made to find out the reasons and circumstances that led to their joining politics and an assessment of their present situation. Apart from obtaining above factual information, the study has been designed mainly to contemplate specific objectives—

1. To study the relationship amongst the political consciousness, political participation and political value in eunuchs of Madhya Pradesh.
2. To find out the relationship amongst age, political consciousness and political participation of the eunuchs of Madhya Pradesh.
3. To study the impact of education on their political consciousness and political participation.
4. To find out the role of media in the changing political consciousness, political participation and political value orientation of the eunuchs of Madhya Pradesh.
5. To study the political consciousness and their participation in politics in terms of place of residence.

## Methodology

The study endeavours some discussions of the factors associated with the way in which eunuchs relate to politics. Explanations related to the attitude of society in a particular situation, discrimination on the basis of gender, discouragement due to sexual incompetence and other related challenges faced by them are usually cited. Thus, the overall strategy is that eunuchs in politics are assessed through various perspectives, some factual, some descriptive, some exploratory and some explanatory. By using eclectic approach, it is not intended to give the impression that any single factor is independent, rather it is clear that all such factors operate in the complex interaction.

## Selection of Respondents

In order to collect the required information for the study and to draw a representative sample of eunuchs, six districts of Madhya Pradesh namely, Bhopal, Gwalior, Jabalpur, Anuppur,

Rewa and Guna have been selected on the basis of concentration of eunuchs who had contested elections so far.

The census treats eunuchs as males and no separate figures in respect to the size of their population are available. Hence, no specific samplıng technique could be adopted. Moreover, eunuchs are generally of a secretive nature and of their own choice inhabit a twilight world of ambiguity. Despite their frequent appearances in public, they trust no one and hate being questioned about their lives, therefore, the selection of respondents very much depended on their willingness to be interviewed. A population of 53 eunuchs were interviewed purposively for the study. The sample consists of only those eunuchs who wear female attire and live in their community, the sample does not include the eunuchs living with their families. No physical check-up has been made in relation to their sexual deformities. Samples were selected merely on the basis of their appearance.

**Data Collection**

The material on which a significant part of this study is based is drawn from the primary data. Primary data were collected through interview-schedules. Two interview-schedules were constructed after obtaining background informations through various secondary sources and through informal interviews with some eunuchs. Secondary data have been gleaned from a wide range of books and journals both Indian and foreign, from internet, newspapers, magazines, etc.

The construction of schedules for the present study was a bit different from other sociological studies as the eunuchs do not belong to either sex, they are hypersensitive, generally have low literacy level and very conservative. Consequently, the construction of schedules depended on various considerations such as objectives of the study, the amount of time at the disposal and convenience of the administration of the schedules. Taking into consideration all the aforementioned factors, two semi-structured interview-schedules—one for analysing the political behaviour of eunuchs in general and another supplementary schedule for those eunuchs who have contested election(s)—were carefully prepared (in Hindi)[2] to measure the various aspects of their political behaviour.

The main interview-schedule has been divided into four sections. Section-I elucidates the personal information of respondents, Section-II deals with the political consciousness of eunuchs, Section-III explores the extent of political participation of eunuchs in the contemporary political realm and Section-IV assesses their political value orientation. The supplementary schedule focuses on the conditions which compel them to join politics, their elections, experiences as politicians, problems encountered during the discharge of duties, attitude of fellow members towards them etc. Before using these schedules on the entire sample, they were pre-tested on a group of eunuchs.

Besides using interview-schedules, observation method, unstructured interviews involving multiple contacts, case studies and photography were also employed to gauge the political behaviour of the eunuchs.

## Difficulties Encountered

During the course of the study, literacy level of eunuchs was a great hurdle in commencing interviews, their conservative nature, dominance of *guru* and hypersensitivity regarding life made the establishment of rapport a difficult task. Considerable amount of time was invested in winning the confidence of prospective eunuchs. Therefore, the timeframe, their community structure, and the budget for the study were the main difficulties encountered during the present study.

## Notes

1. In India, for a long time, the existence of eunuchs as a group was not recognised by the law. After a long struggle under the banner of *All India Hijra Kalyan Sabha,* which was formed in 1983, eunuchs were granted voting rights by the Supreme Court of India in 1986. But due to their ambiguous sexual identity it did not come to practice

and after a long debate, the Delhi Election Office left it to the eunuchs to decide whether they want their names registered in the voters list as males or females (*Indian Express*, 3 November 1994).

2. The eunuchs have no special language of their own but they communicate either in Hindi or the regional language to which they belong. Hence, the interviews have been carried out in Hindi which is my native language.

# Two

# Some Important Works on Eunuchs

## A Review

Eunuchs have always been an integral part of Indian society. It is very difficult to trace its first emergence in the society, as the concept of androgyny *(Ardhanarishvara)*[1] is well known in the Hindu mythology. Similarly, the Greek mythology refers to a being–partly male, partly female—called *Hermaphroditus*.[2] Hermaphrodite[3] can be recognised as androgyny. But the definition of eunuch changed from theosophical to practical, when the tradition of castration or emasculation started in the society, may be due to various causes from social punishment to criminal ones. The motive behind the castration has always been making an individual sexually incomplete so that he cannot procreate. Eunuchs view 'the operation of emasculation' as a procedure by which a special power emerges when the male dies and is replaced with a new person, someone not male and not wholly female either. Thus, the word eunuchs which literally means impotent men, consist of hermaphrodites as well as castrated ones.

Though the exact date about the initiation of castration is still an unsolved question, yet, *Encyclopaedia of Religion and Ethics* (Vol. V, 1981) states that it was first instituted by the Semiramis of Mesopotamian region.[4] History mentions the tradition of making and keeping eunuchs in European countries (white eunuchs) like Spain, Greece, Rome, Russia, etc., in African countries (black or negro eunuchs) like Syria, Morocco, Egypt, Sudan and even in Asia major and Asia minor i.e. in China, India, Pakistan, Bangladesh, Saudi Arab, Iraq, etc. Thus, the eunuchs existed throughout the world. With the advent of time, in the western countries, eunuchs lost their identity, but in eastern countries especially the middle-east and south-eastern Asian countries, society allotted some social and cultural space to this particular minority of eunuchs.

There are numerous references of eunuchs in the Indian classics which depict that during vedic period human males were castrated and were called *Vadhris* (*Atharvaveda*, vi, cxxxviii, 2). During this period eunuchs used to sing and dance for their livelihood *(Atharvaveda,* viii, vi, 11, *Mahabharata* III, xlvi) and their status in society was the lowest. They were not included in any *varna,* and special rules were framed for them.[5] They were treated as untouchables.[6] During the 2nd and the 5th century A.D. eunuchs were employed in royal courts and guards of *Antahpura.*[7] Legendary Arjuna did similar service disguised as Vrihannala (a eunuch) at the palace of king Virata during his exile. At the same time, we find reference of Shikhandi (a born eunuch), a maternal uncle of Kauravas, who played the key role in the battle of *Mahabharata*. Perhaps

Shikhandi was the person who could be perceived as political advisor of Kauravas.[8]

Throughout the world whether it is Asia, Africa or Europe, eunuchs were employed as guards of bed chambers, guards of royal kitchens and as slaves in general. Some beautiful eunuchs were kept for sodomy, besides these some wise and shrewd eunuchs played important roles in many royal courts. According to Saletore (1974), the eunuchs continued to be notable features of the medieval courts in India. During this period, they were the privileged ones. Many offices like Vijayanagar court[9], Ala-ud-din Khilji's court[10] and the Mughal courts, were however explicitly associated with slave-eunuchs, or Khwajaserai[11]. The eunuchs in Mughal Empire enjoyed power and proved their administrative skills. A historian, Lal (1988) mentioned that many administrators like Firoz Khan, Hilal Khan, I'tihar Khan and some other eunuchs ruled different territories of the Mughal Empire. Unfortunately historians acclaimed only these trustworthies of Mughal reign which were very less in number, whereas thousands of men were emasculated throughout the country, and led very miserable life of slaves and servants[12].

The practice of employing eunuchs continued till the 18th and 19th centuries until the decline of Mughal Empire. The royal families virtually became impoverished, they threw eunuchs out of their houses. Abashed eunuchs came together for the first time for protection[13]. They started living together as an organised community. After being ostracised and despised by the society from centuries, they learnt to conceal their seductive charms under a mask of repulsive ugliness. They became conservative about themselves as well as about their rites. Their secretive nature attracted scholars to unveil the shroud from the community. The story of the mechanism of recruitment, socialization, their rituals and mode of social control has been narrated by many anthropologists, sociologists and historians.

Faridi (1899), Thurston and Rangachari (1909), Russell and Hiralal (1916), Mehta (1947), Shah (1961) and Salunke (1976) highlighted the community life of eunuchs. They all described the process of emasculation as an integral part of their works. Raghuvanshi and Navalkar (1980) also wrote about their living, initiation and death. Interestingly, almost all the above scholars mentioned the same mode of emasculation, to which eunuchs call *nirvana*. Vyas and Shingala (1987) studied the lifestyle of eunuchs of Baroda (Gujarat) empirically (perhaps for the first time). Sinha (1967) described the mode of socialization of neophyte in the eunuch community of Lucknow (the capital of Uttar Pradesh). He explained the stages of metamorphosis through which a novice becomes a fully-fledged eunuch. Cohen (1995) studied eunuchs and *Jankhas* (transvestite) and commented on castration as 'castration of desire'.

Some scholars like Salunke (1976), Ranade (1983) and Vyas and Shingala (1987) revealed the reasons which motivate people to join the eunuch community. The common reasons which they disclosed are indeterminate sex, impotency, religious frenzy, strong drive for becoming woman, forced castration etc. Whatever be the cause, the fact remains that approximately 40,000 boys and young men are castrated each year in the country[14] (*The Weekend Observer*, 23 October 1993; *The Hindustan Times*, 14 March 1994).

A cultural anthropologist, Nanda (1990) identified eunuchs as religious, and followers of the *Bahuchara Mata*. She also tried to explain their gender identity with the view that *hijras* (eunuchs) may reasonably be described as institutionalised third gender. This institutionalisation of the eunuchs is indicated by the fact that like any other social organisation, they do have a code of conduct, a value system, specific style of living and the like to justify their right to exist.[15] They have their own panchayat to resolve their disputes. Another important feature of this community is their language despite having no special language of the community, they speak their regional language or their mother tongue. The grammar is generally feminine as they imitate women in speech. They use some vulgar terms and expressions in their speech, which reflect on their private lives. Almost all the terms they use are connected with their homo sexual experiences.[16]

Hall, a linguist deciphered the relationship of language and identity construction among eunuchs in India. Her work talks about the way sexuality and gender is negotiated in language. According to Hall (1997), eunuchs use devices like different use of gender markings, mannerisms, verbal insults etc. to convey the fluidity of identity.

Psychological studies reveal their lexis, body language, mannerisms and behaviour with their own cognizance. According to Ayub and Khan (1988) and Khan and Ayub (2002), since childhood, eunuchs face many hardships in their lives. Deprived from the native family, eunuchs confront with many problems like sexual incompleteness, sexual urge, humiliation and intolerance from the society. All these affect their personality, resulting in adopting many defense mechanisms like high needs for abasement and aggression and low needs for achievement and counteraction. This leads them to be aggressive, pessimistic and un-ambitious. Their feelings of insecurity brought them together, closer, and made them organised and well knit. With unique customs and traditions, eunuchs propounded themselves as the third gender and are legitimated by the Indian society.

Though eunuchs had always been jeered and disgraced due to their sexual handicappedness yet their every behaviour in the society is scrutinized and talked about. With the growing hostility in an increasing modern society, the older order breaking down and with the erosion of belief that they have occult power to confer prosperity and health on new-born babies and newly-wed couples ensued in constriction of their earnings. Devastated eunuchs have searched many alternative sources of income like—prostitution, smuggling of kidney (*Anand Bazar Patrika,* 23 March 1995), drug trafficking (*Anand Bazar Patrika,* 29 March 1995) etc.

In this endeavour of re-inventing themselves, the involvement and the victory of eunuchs in elections marked step towards social acceptance for a community that has been reviled for centuries and has given fresh impetus to the fight for their rights in the democratic India. This was something which has never ever happened so far in the country and was documented with great fanaticism. The success of few eunuchs in politics was not an overnight achievement as was highlighted in the media rather there is a long story of suffrage behind it.

Besides few research articles on the empowerment of eunuchs, their political behaviour has not yet been studied empirically. Satyal (2001) in her article 'Hijras and the Politics of Empowerment in Contemporary India' indicates that the 'birth' of the *hijra* (eunuch) as a politician spans various temporalities. They have acted as a political metaphor and in the process lent a paradoxical twist to the meanings of the very symbols of which the *hijra* is a repository. Indeed, the *hijras* struggle to various positions and discourses and serve to emphasize the complexities of the 'modern' and the politics of democracy in India.

Recently, the work of Reddy (2003) with the enticing title of 'Men who would be kings' questioned automatically presumed relationship between *hijra* marginalisation and their social emancipation by virtue of electoral participation. Accordingly, to gain political status, *hijras* are entering the public imagination, explicitly highlighting their social marginality on the basis of their sexuality, religion and kinship. She argued that *hijras* apparent increase in political visibility and social status could be illusory and could ultimately serve to re-marginalise them within the new social order.

Although the quantitative study of political behaviour was started in the 1920s, the first systematic study was done in 1940 in the USA during Presidential elections by Paul F. Lazarsfeld, Bernard Berelson and Hazel Gaudet. On analysing the political behaviour quantitatively, Butler (1958:71) raised questions on the accuracy in the measurement which is one of the basic elements of scientific method. In the study of political behaviour it is very difficult to deal with all variables and it is also not possible to reduce all political problems to figures.

Since facts are objective and verifiable, Butler (1958) puts them in four categories. The approaches are—deductive, descriptive, quantitative and sociological and psychological approach. In deductive approach man's political and social instincts are deduced. The conclusions generated from such assumptions are far from the realities. Descriptive approach is based on the first hand information obtained either from observation, interviews or from the documents available. Nothing definitive about the conclusions based on this approach has been claimed by the followers of this approach. In quantitative approach, statistics is applied to analyse the data. It has also been argued that the quantification of information can support and supplement a descriptive statement, whereas in sociological and psychological approach, relationship between social class and voting behaviour is studied. Mills (1956) in the study of power elite, attempted to identify the most influential people in American society, their characteristics and their methods of wielding authority. This study is considered one of the leading contributions by the sociologists to the study of political behaviour.

Now-a-days, an eclectic approach is generally adopted by the scholars to study the political behaviour. In democratic society elections provide the only opportunity when the people exercise their power to elect their representative, and for the researches it is the time when their behaviour in electoral politics is gauged by various approaches and techniques. Peterson (1990) suggested a model of political behaviour which sees the role of different variables and their effect on people's political behaviour.

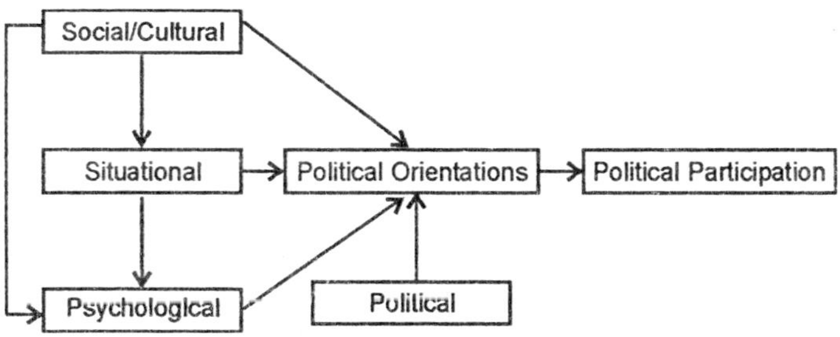


This model combines the Socio-Economic Status model (Verba and Nie, 1972) with recognition of the role of psychological variables as intervening between SES and political orientation. According to Peterson, socio-economic factors along with two variables i.e., political variable and situational variable are conceived as exogenous and events from the larger political system, whereas, situational variables are the events from everyday life like stress, health and nutritional problems, sexual abuse, death anxiety and experience, work place, media, etc.

It has also been opined that political behaviour is the function of two factors—internal and environmental stimuli. Accordingly, the influence of groups, circumstances of one's life, educational level, socio-economic status, interpersonal relationships, cross-pressures of the groups etc. are the various environmental factors which influence the political behaviour of human beings, whereas, physical appearance, image, past experience, mental ability to handle particular situation, etc. are some internal factors which have dramatic implications for political behaviour (Jaros and Grant, 1974). The situation is illustrated by the diagram below.

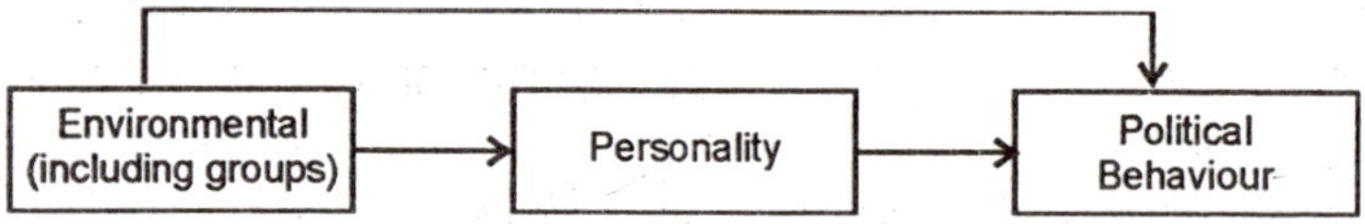


According to Jaros and Grant, environment shapes personality which in turn shapes behaviour. In casual parlance we may identify personality which intervenes between environment and behaviour.

Interestingly, the review of literature of political behaviour studies reveals that no two scholars have used the same measures to analyse political behaviour. Social scientists in India began empirical studies of political behaviour at the time of the third general elections in 1962, as the first two general elections held in 1952 and 1957 did not attract social scientists.[17] The same election motivated many sociologists and political scientists to study the behaviour of mass. The study of Sirsikar (1965) was the first empirical study of political behaviour in India. 1258 people were interviewed in Pune city in order to study the voting behaviour in a systematic manner. Sirsikar analysed the impact of the socio-economic backgrounds of voters on various aspects of political behaviour separately but didn't prepare any scale.

The study of the fourth general elections conducted by Atal (1971) is considered important and different one because he not only interviewed a group of people twice or thrice before and after the polling was over but also analysed the data and developed various indices to measure the voting behaviour such as: (i) exposure to mass-media, (ii) political awareness, (iii) political opinion, (iv) political participation, and (v) political efficacy. Like Atal, Verma and Iqbal Narain and others (1973) also studied voting behaviour in 1967. They ascertained voting behaviour on the basis of political information, media of communication, exposure to campaign, purpose of voting and political efficacy. Both Atal and Verma *et al.* constructed their own scales, scoring keys (on the basis of weightage) and classified the sample population into high, medium and low.

It is observed that for the two decades or so all elections whether it is local, state or general elections are highlighted by the media. Research institutes and mass-media are accomplishing public opinion surveys, pre-post poll analysis, etc. and concentrating on the micro-analysis of the contribution, viewpoint, attitude or behaviour of specific caste, community, religion, etc. in the elections.

The eunuch community that had been subdued for centuries, animated and challenged the supremacy of the male stream in various elections. After a long struggle, in 1986, through the Supreme Court of India the community acquired their dignity and suffrage (*The Telegraph*, 31 July 1994).Till 1998, the situation transmogrified, the community that was living on the fringes of society forayed into the political domain. Vinayak (1998) documented few eunuch politicians of Punjab, Haryana and Rajasthan and remarked "their success as an identity earned through their no-nonsense approach" (Out of the Shadows. *India Today*, March 21, 1998, p. 10). But the success of these eunuchs had been considered as coincidence and they were ignored. Within two years the scenario erupted in Madhya Pradesh too, when eunuchs started striking the headlines. The story began with the victory of Kamala Jaan who became the first eunuch Mayor of Katni, M.P., then Shabnam Mausi elected to the post of M.L.A. from Sohagpur of district Shahdol. Since then more than half a dozen eunuchs have confronted the mainstream political discourse in Madhya Pradesh and after each victory their candidatures have been questioned. The present study will add to the existing scholarship on the political empowerment of eunuchs by analysing their political behaviour empirically.

## Notes

1. *Ardhanarishvara* manifested the characteristics of both sexes. Half male i.e. of Lord Shiva—*Ardha-nara,* and half female i.e. of Goddess Parvati—*Ardha-nari.*
2. It is believed that *Hermaphroditus,* the son of Greek God *Hermes* (Mercury) and Goddess *Aphrodite* (Venus) a very handsome man was once bathing in a fountain. The nymph of fountain became enamoured and sought God a permanent unity. Thus, *Hermaphroditus* became half male and half female.
3. *Hermaphrodites* consist of both male and female sex organs. Due to their ambiguous sex they become sexually handicapped and are known as eunuchs.
4. In his work *Born Eunuchs: Homosexual Identity in the Ancient World* (1999), Faris Malik notes that the overwhelming number of sources failing to specify that the practice of castrating innocent young men and boys was started by a legendary Assyrian queen Semiramis. This tradition may be based on the myth of Cybele and Attis, in which Attis refused to sleep with Cybele and was castrated by her for his refusal.
   I am not concerned with Cybele—*Attis cult,* nor does my inquiry touch religious eunuchs. The mention of the existence of such strange cult is to show how this myth is paralleled in the Indian story of Arjuna in the *Mahabharata.* Arjuna, the mighty warrior, was cursed with impotence by Urvasi because he refused to sleep with her. Indra reduced Arjuna's period of impotence to one year and he spent his year as a eunuch Vrihannala. *See* also *Van Buitenen,* 1984.
5. The Hindu jurists and compilers of *Dharmashastra* framed rules relating to duty, marriage, divorce, chastity, *niyoga,* inheritance, maintenance, food stuffs, religious matters, sacrifices, auspicious omen, disabilities and privileges of the four *varnas* and mixed castes, for example, in the *Manusmriti,* although clearly viewed in a pejorative light. Characteristically, the *Arthashastra* views them from a more practical point of view. See R.P. Kangle: *Kautilya's Arthasastra,* 2 vols. Bombay, 1960-63.

6. Manu, iii, 165.
7. *Antahpuras* were the royal lodging of ladies where entrance of men was restricted. Eunuchs were employed here for strict vigilance, safety and entertainment.
8. See, for example, Mitamura (1970), and Anderson (1990) for discussions of political functions of eunuchs in China.
   Eunuchs functioned as political advisors in China as early as the Chau Period (1122-221 B.C.) and continued as such under various dynasties until the end of imperial regime. Even in Persia, Rome, Byzantine, etc. eunuchs acted as political advisors and even ruled the countries. Many of the details described here for Chinese eunuchs are similar to the political functions of Shikhandi in *Mahabharata.*
9. As has often been noted, the demand for eunuchs in India was undoubtedly very popular till medieval period. First and foremost, they were required as guardians of the womenfolk, affluent enough to be able to maintain a *harem.* They were much sought after as confidential servants, to watch over their masters'/mistresses' interests. In the Vijayanagar Kingdom, each of the queen's houses debarred the entrance of any man with the exception of eunuchs (*See* Saletore, 1974:196-98).
10. The Khiljis ruled from 1290-1320 A.D. and during this period the importance of the eunuchs *(Khwajaseras)* in the court at Delhi probably reached its peak, especially during the reign of Ala-ud-din Khilji. There is an outstanding example of a eunuch Malik Kafur, who first served as an intimate slave and thereafter became the *wazir* in Ala-ud-din's army.
11. *Khwajaserai* is the Persian equivalent of the eunuchs. In the institution of *Khwajaseras* eunuchs controlled the organisational affairs in the Mughal period. They also acted as cast spells in the Mughal courts. Later on it became a title for administrative officer of the *harems.*
12. For a useful, concise description of the trade in eunuchs in Mughal Bengal, see Hambly (1974).
13. For the provocative discussion on the curious position of the eunuchs in Indian society, *see* Dalrymple (1992) and Chatterjee (1999).
14. Previously the rite of emasculation was performed in the temple of Bahuchara Mata (The goddess worshipped by the eunuchs) which is situated at Sankhalpur, 60 km away from Ahmedabad (Gujarat), but now to avoid police surveillance is conducted clandestinely.
    During my studies in Madhya Pradesh, I have observed that many eunuchs do not speak of this sacrifice (emasculation) but rather insist that they were born hermaphrodites. It is difficult to ascertain the truth about these claims, yet stories of such births are rare. In the villages of central India and in north India too, it is believed that all children born with ambiguous genital are the property of the eunuchs, to be raised by them. In reality, (most, if not all) join the

eunuch community as adolescents or adults. It is not unusual to hear from the eunuchs that since her birth, she felt like a girl in childhood, gradually she discovered that she was different and other children started making fun of her, she was raised as a girl by her parents, married off to a man, who on the wedding night discovered her dual genitals, threw her out which left her with no other alternative but to leave the family and perhaps join a eunuch community to earn a living.

Such disdain many be due to the fact that for a society like India, where reproduction is highly valued for both men and women, the eunuchs' impotence stigmatizes them as useless. Their birth is a source of sorrow for the family and their presence is generally considered a burden on the family. The reason many eunuchs give for joining the community is to relieve their families of the embarrassment of their presence.

15. Eunuchs who dress and act like women have been a presence in India for generations. Within South Asian Society they maintain a third-gender role that has become institutionalised through tradition. They often live in close communities and set up their own family networks of motherhood, daughterhood and sisterhood. All eunuchs have to find a *guru* (mentor) to sponsor them by paying their *dand* (fine) before they are accepted into the community (Bakshi, 2004:213). The initiation fine is comparable to a dowry because the *dand*, which is slowly paid off by the eunuchs, is meant to ensure safety and stability with the new community.

    As a matter of fact, every eunuch comes from a different cultural background and becomes a life member of some *Akhada, Math* or *Dayra*, where they live as a group and have a strong bond of sympathy with each other. It is the common abnormality of sexual incompetence and impotence which creates a strong bond of affinity amongst them. The head of the clan is usually called *nayak* or *guru* (a cult figure revered by the eunuch community). It is generally said that there is a hierarchy between *chelas* and *gurus*, but their relationship is not necessarily seen as a negative relationship. New entrants are in charge of household chores but in exchange of their work, *gurus* look after and protect them (Nanda, 2002:162).

16. The psychological explanation of using obscene language seems to be that as the normal sex is denied to the eunuchs. They talk about it whenever they get an opportunity. This denial haunts their minds and hence it is reflected in their language and expressions.

17. The credit of introducing survey research in political science in India goes to Rajni Kothari whose Centre for the Study of Developing Societies (CSDS) conducted election surveys. The centre is still continuing with the election surveys and analysis.

# THREE
# Political Functions of Eunuchs in Retrospect

Eunuchs have been recognised as nature's freaks, howsoever, their role in the society has changed over the centuries. While the androgyne *(Ardhanarishvara)* has been adored as divine figure, the human embodiments of sexual and gender atypicality (acquired by birth or through emasculation) seem to have been generally accorded a rather low or even despised status in the society.

Eunuchs in antiquity were the need of the plutocrats. They were supposed to be dependable harem guards, body guards, chamberlains, laborious servants and agricultural slaves. But the origin of a phenomenon does not explain its persistence or its transformation [Durkheim (1950:97)]. Being socially rootless[1], eunuchs were employed in domestic as well as political servitude. Coser (1964:881) explained the need of political eunuchism. Accordingly, the emperor wished to minimise his dependency on the bureaucracy, whose impersonal standards made it insufficiently pliable as an instrument of personal rule. He therefore, required men who would owe him total allegiance. The tension between the need to rely on bureaucracy for purposes of centralization and the need for personal allegiance and dependence led to the creation of a new role, that of the political eunuchs.

The recent political behaviour of eunuchs in the political scenario of Madhya Pradesh is not an accidental eruption (as it was highlighted in the media). They have always been politically active in some way or the other. To clear the danger of anachronism, some factual data have been gleaned from wide range of literature depicting the political functions of eunuchs from antiquity to the pre-modern society throughout the world.

Eunuchs were well known in the ancient Assyria even in the 2nd millennium B.C. They acted as Generals and Governors. Queen Semiramis of Assyria who had conquered many lands had a large troop of eunuchs. From Babylon and Assyria, the atrocity of castration was introduced to Persia, where the eunuchs became an institution. They were given very high positions in the Persian Court of King Darius. During this period eunuchs were supposed to be valuable presents with which one king used to oblige the other king. Rawlinson (2001:221) reported that in Persia, after Xerxes, the eunuchs acquired a vast political authority and appeared to have filled all the chief offices of states. They were the king's advisors in the palace and generals in the field. They superintended the education of the young princes and found it easy to make them their tools.[2]

The custom of employing eunuchs as servants was popular in Israel at least as early as the reign of Jehu, in Greece by the time of Persian wars, in Egypt during the XX dynasty (1202-1102 B.C.), it reached its epitome at the court of Constantinople under the Byzantine emperors. They often rose to high position, the Byzantine general *Narses* being the most celebrated one (*Encyclopaedia of Religion and Ethics,* 1981:580).

In the Mamluk sultanate eunuchs were extremely important and vital elements in the Mamluk military aristocracy in spite of being handicapped by two great drawbacks: (a) they hardly ever constituted a cohesive body fighting for their own material or political interests, (b) none of them could attain ranks or positions of power and influence comparable to those attained by the eunuchs in Islam in previous periods, almost upto the end of the Ayyubid rule (Ayalon, 1977:268)[3]. Eunuchs during this period were called 'Men of the Sword' (*arbab al-suyuf*). Eunuchs usually served as Sultan's elite body guards, retinue or as cupbearers, grand treasurers, educators as well as guardian of Sultan's children. Another important role of eunuchs in Mamluk Sultanate was the distribution of fiefs, which was the main source of income for the military aristocracy (*Ibid*: 288).

After conquering Mamluk Sultanate, Ottoman Empire ruled over the entire Middle East and Eastern Europe for nearly five centuries. Toledano (1984:382) revealed that throughout their lives the eunuchs suffered hormonal and psychological disorders and were said to have developed peculiar characteristics and an eccentric social behaviour. This has special significance since senior eunuchs had access to power and during certain periods of the Ottoman history, exercised it to influence the course of political events. During the second half of the period between the sixteenth century and the eighteenth century, the African eunuchs became powerful at the Ottoman Court. Ulucay, who surveyed the influence of African eunuchs calls this period as 'Sultanate of the African Eunuchs'. He also attributes the decline and fall of the Empire to the corrupting role played by the eunuchs at the court. By the end of the medieval period military slavery and agricultural slavery ended but the household slavery persisted till the nineteenth century.

Coser (1964:881-882) on the one hand asserted that bureaucratic officials were exceedingly distrustful of the eunuch system because it negated the emphasis on rationality and on disciplined and methodical behaviour, which is the very essence of expert officialdom. On the other hand, while discussing political eunuchism of the Chinese eunuchs, he stated that though socially rootless, eunuchs remained preferred instruments of rulers.

According to Weber (1951:138), it is very difficult to understand Chinese history without knowing the constant struggle between the literati and the eunuch system in China. Eunuchs became a part of Chinese court by the first millennium B.C. They were employed as political advisors in China during Chou period (1122-221 B.C.). In Qin's dynasty and in Han dynasty (202 B.C.-220 A.D.) the position of eunuchs became very strong in the imperial courts.[4] In Ming China whole departments of eunuchs came into existence at court and were soon made use of confidential business of the emperor outside the palace (Eberhard, 1960:253). They headed armies at times, controlled the bureaucracy so that counsellors could communicate with emperor only through the intermediary of eunuchs (Weber, 1951:285). During T'ang dynasty political eunuchism grew under the autocratic system. Throughout Chinese history eunuchs have been associated with arrogance, suspicion, cunningness, greed, gluttony and a love for luxury.

## The Eunuchs in India

The status of eunuchs in the Indian sub-continent was more or less analogous to the rest of the world. They became a permanent feature of Hindu court life from very early times (the existence of the eunuchs in the palace and outside has previously been pointed out at some length), according to Kautilya, eunuchs in the 4th century B.C. were employed in the court of Chandragupta Maurya to regulate the affairs of the *antahpura* (inner apartments) of the palaces to the satisfaction of the king and other specified duties assigned to them. This may be true for the handful of eunuchs, but the majority of them belonged to the lower social strata where they were treated on par with the animals. The purpose of this chapter is to focus on those elite eunuchs who enjoyed special social status and unique social positions in the courts.

During the Khilji dynasty (1290-1320 A.D.) eunuchs began to interfere in the court politics and even participated in battles and conquests. We find a eunuch by the name Malik Kafur in the court of Ala-ud-din Khilji (1296-1315 A.D.). Ala-ud-din had become infatuated with this extremely handsome young boy and had purchased him for one thousand dinars and later on this slave also came to be known as *hazar dinari*. Very soon this slave was appointed as senior commander in the King's army. Later on he became the *Wazir* (Prime Minister).[5] After the death of Ala-ud-din Khilji, guileful Malik Kafur managed to raise the minor son of Ala-ud-din to the throne and acquired all powers safely in his hands.

Malik Sarwar was another star eunuch who proved his administrative skills in the Tughlaq dynasty. Initially Sarwar was custodian of the royal jewellery in the Sultan Firuz Shah Tughlaq (1351-1388 A.D.). During the reign of Muhammad Shah, Malik Sarwar was appointed as *Wazir* and got the title of *Khwaja-i-Jahan*. Muhammad Shah entrusted the eastern districts to Sarwar and conferred the title of *Sultan-ush- Sharq* on him. Muhammad Shah's son Humayun Khan and his grandson Sultan Mahmud recognized the ability of Malik Sarwar and gave the responsibilities of the entire administration of eastern districts to him and appointed him Governor in 1394 (Habib and Nizami, 1970; Saeed, 1972). Thus, Malik Sarwar Sultan-ush-Sharq founded 'the Sharqi Kingdom' at Jaunpur and ruled eastern districts like Jaunpur, Rae Bareli, Bara Banki, Aligarh, Moradabad, Mainpuri, etc. from 1394-1399. His[6] great administrative talents coupled with his grim political realism and military efficiency raised his stature immensely. He established law and order in areas which were seething with discontent and brought the recalcitrant *Zamindars* under submission.

Eunuchs during Mughals were known as *Khwajaseras* and were appointed on guard duty in the *harems*, administrators, governors and army commanders. Some learned eunuchs used to teach 'the liberal and military arts' to the princes (Lal, 1988:113). Eunuchs were stratified in Mughal period, the senior eunuchs were called *Nazirs.* The Chief *Nazirs* were entitled as Aitmad or Aitwar Khan (the trusted Lord). Each of these had number of other eunuchs under them. History narrates that one Aitwar Khan was in the service of Babur and Humayun. In the second year of Akbar's reign he chaperoned Akbar's mother and other Begams from Kabul to Hindustan. Later on he was rewarded with the appointment as Governor of Delhi. Another eunuch Phool Malik, also known as Muhammad Khan, was given responsibility to improve the damaged finances during the reign of Akbar. One Aitmad Khan built the town Itmadpur near Agra, *Khwajasera* Hilal, a eunuch who joined Jahangir's service built another town Hilallabad. One finds another monument on Gwalior-Agra road at Agra, known as the 'Tomb of Feroze Khan'. This eunuch (Feroze Khan) was also the founder of Ferozabad town (Sharma, 1984:384). Similarly, Bakhtawar Khan, superintendent of the eunuchs under Aurangzeb, held the rank of *hazari.*

Many *Khwajaseras* and *Nazirs* thus were best qualified for their trust as they had no separate identity from their masters. As surrogates of masters, (either kings or queens), they could wield great influence in government and politics. During the later Mughal period three eunuchs, Mian Khushfahan, Mian Arjmand and Mian Mahabat ruled the declining state on behalf of Mughalani Begum, the Governor of Lahore (1754-1756) [Sarkar, 1964:440].

The persistent association of eunuchs with specific offices according to their capabilities in the administration of various Indian polities was no coincidence rather a trend. We also get references of eunuch officials in the Nizamat records of Murshidabad (now in West Bengal) during the eighteenth century. The eunuch Ambar is listed as Darogha *Mashalkhana* in the household list of 1772, Ghulam Muhammad Khan is described as Darogha *Mir Shikaran.* Eunuchs also held offices like Darogha *Nawarrah* (boats). Many eunuchs were employed in *qalamdankhana,* an office through which the wealth of the house was governed where they used to supervise Nizamat treasury, accountants and administered the profits arising from trade and the collections of the various revenue-farms. One eunuch Siddi Ambar Ali Khan, Darogha of *qalamdankhana* was appointed to teach finance management to the nobles (Chatterjee, 1999: 47). Another eunuch who came in bride's dowry with *Bahu Begum* when she married Shuja-ud-daula, managed her estates in Gonda and Faizabad (Barnett, 1987:182). Similarly, in the Nizamat, in 1772-1773, after the accession of a young Mubarak-ud-daula I, and during the regency of Manni Begum, the eunuch Itibar Khan, proved to be much more powerful than the *Nazims* (Chatterjee, 1999:50).

In the early 19th century, eunuchs always enjoyed a special status in Lucknow, the city of Nawabs. When Nawab Nasiruddin Haider ruled Awadh (1827-1837 A.D.) with Lucknow as his capital, eunuchs had acquired not only a special status but had a typical role in the monarchy. They were part of Muslim aristocracy and were found in large numbers in the mansions of the aristocracy. Generally, they were not treated at par with human beings though a few of them were good at winning the hearts of their masters and on occasions used to be close confidents. In the palace of the Nawab, there were not less than 150 eunuchs at any given time. The chief eunuch was in the personal service of the Begum and had a lot of clout in the court of Awadh (Ali, 1974). Many of the eunuchs were advanced to high offices of trust under the Awadh government. Once the Nawab gave a few prosperous districts to one of his eunuchs, he was governing as well as collecting the revenue for the Nawab from his area. Over a period of time, he amassed unimaginable wealth and started living in a palace with his personal army (Bhatt, 2006). Generally, Nawabs and rich persons were over generous in giving valuable gifts to the slaves for even unimportant reasons. One reason could be because, slaves were the property of masters and the slaves did not have inheritance rights.

When the Mughal court was disbanded, the plutocratics were ruined and became impecunious to afford luxuries like slaves or eunuchs. Moreover, after Mughals, disintegrated kingdoms were struggling for their existence against the British rule. Even the British government did not like the presence of eunuchs in the society. They tried to abolish them by banning the castration.[6] Though the British failed in their attempts to control and curtail the eunuchs, the eunuchs once again, became insecure socially as well as emotionally.

Thrown out of their homes, rejected by their families, eunuchs in the 20th century came together for protection. They started living in a community with their own norms and rituals. They struggled and are struggling for their social and political emancipation which will be discussed in the next chapter.

## Notes

1. After joining the eunuch community, individuals have to leave their native families. Generally, they do not maintain any contact with their natal families and the families too, in most cases, are not anxious to retain any contact with them because their presence is generally considered useless, stigmatised and a burden.
2. According to *Encyclopaedia of Islam* (Vol. IV, 1978:1092), in Persia, it was only under the Safawids that the eunuchs in charge of the women's apartments in the royal palace began to play an important role in political affairs. Shah Abbas (1587-1629) was the first Shah to introduce white eunuchs into the palace alongside the black eunuchs. He also initiated the practice of immuring the royal princes in the harem. This practice unfitted the princes for rule and in due course enabled the palace eunuchs to dominate affairs of state. On the death of Shah Abbas II in 1667, the palace eunuchs contrived the succession of Shah Sulayman and seized control of the state. Thereafter, Shah Sultan Husayn was placed on the throne. He left the management of affairs of state entirely to them. They succeeded in extending their influence over military as well as civil affairs. In due course, the irresponsible character of their government and the faction which prevailed in their own ranks led to the decline of Safawid dynasty. And after the fall of Safawids, the eunuchs never again achieved political importance. For a relevant, concise description of Safawid dynasty, see Lockhart (1958).
3. The works of Ayalon (1977) and Marmon (1995) give an account of the Mamluk officer corps which consisted of three ranks: Amir of a Hundred, Amir of Forty and Amir of Ten. It has been stated that though no eunuch rose to the rank of 'Amir of Hundred' in the

sultanate, without eunuchs in the military school the Mamluk Military Aristocracy could not have functioned properly.

4. To meet the demand some individuals used to castrate voluntarily and some parents used to castrate their children just to get some position in the imperial court (Wittfogel, 1963:356). In these cases political eunuchism was not complete in true sense. The eunuchs remained preferred instruments of rulers, because they could have no issue to harbour, but being attached to native families, they could not serve their masters with the same dedication as the eunuchs who were socially rootless served.
5. Ala-ud-din Khilji was famous for his ardour for homosexuality and his insane passion for Malik Kafur was widely known. The sycophant Malik Kafur knew his effeminate characteristics captivated the Sultan completely and managed to acquire powers.
6. During medieval period eunuchs were designated with masculine names and masculine personal pronouns were used for them, but now-a-days they have feminine names and use feminine gender for themselves.
7. For more information see, *Pune Archives*: XIV, 8/94; fols 13-17, R.D. Luard, Subcollector to R. Mills, Collector of Pune, 14 Nov. 1836; *Pune Archives*: XIV; 8/94, fols 11-12, R. Mills, Collector of Pune to W. Williamson, Revenue Commissioner, 28 Nov. 1836; Pune Archives: XIV; 8/94, fols 17-18, R.T. Webb, Registrar of Sardar Faujdari Adalat to Government, 2 May 1837.

# FOUR
# Struggle for Political Emancipation

Till the 20th century the society was totally absorbed by the two-gender model. The existence of the third gender in the Indian society was completely ignored. The eunuchs who were part of the mainstream of the medieval period, were compelled to live on the fringes of Indian society. Ostracized by the society, eunuchs communed to combat their social, economic and emotional insecurity.[1] Their sexual incompleteness always led them to humiliation and abasement in the society. For emotional security they entered into fake interpersonal relationships like *bahin, mausi, dadi, nani,* etc. Since they have no opportunity to celebrate traditional social events like a wedding or the birth of a child, eunuchs have invented a few ceremonies of their own: *bahin banana* (to make someone a sister) or *beti banana* (to adopt a daughter). These occasions, celebrated on the same scale as marriages, form new relationships for them.

Insecure eunuchs live together in a place called *akhada* or *dayra*. The members of a *dayra* form a corporate unit with its own property and income—expenditure. Each *akhada* or *dayra* has a definite jurisdiction i.e., a definite territory—villages or towns or colonies of towns—where the members usually collect alms. After deducting the joint expenses of the *dayra*, eunuchs distribute their earnings among themselves. The head of the *akhada*, who is called *nayak* or *guru* (mentor) gets the largest share. In turn *guru* takes care of them, sustains them and understands them. The *guru* exercises absolute control over the *chelas* (disciples), even to the extent of deciding who they may talk to. Therefore, the authority of the *guru* is respected and accepted by the members of the *akhada/dayra/gaddi*.[2] The formation of these relationships signifies interdependence for the fulfilment of certain needs and also for socio-economic and psychological security. The organised living not only diminishes disharmony among the members of the community but also creates a 'we' feeling.

Here, it should be noted that the authority of the *guru* or *nayak* extends to those eunuchs also who prefer to live away from *akhada*. The rules and regulations of the community are applicable to all the eunuchs including those who do not live in the *akhada*, and they too have to cooperate in all the social, economic and religious activities.

The community has their own *Panchayat* (council) to settle any disputes over earnings, to avoid turf battles, to fine the accused, etc. The decisions of the *Panchayat* have to be accepted by the entire community. The *Panchayat* functions by virtue of the general agreement and as long as the pleasure of the community lasts. It sustains the social norms, rites, rituals and protects the community from any kind of threat. The verdict of the *Panchayat* is final, over which there is no appeal. As mentioned earlier, the *Panchayat* has the ultimate power to punish or fine a culprit and in most cases, they exercise their power. The few rebellions that are highlighted in the media mostly are due to the hunger for power and money. In some cases these rebellions arise because of the *panchayat's* failure to resolve their disputes.

As the lifestyle of people is changing in the modern society, the perils within and outside the eunuch community are also changing its yardsticks. In order to acclimatise in the contemporary social panorama, the eunuchs are deviating from their traditional occupation. They say family planning and a growing hostility towards the belief that eunuchs bring good luck at weddings or a birth, are threatening their existence.

The personality analysis of eunuchs shows high abasement, need for nurturance and succorance towards them than the normal individuals (Ayub and Khan, 1998). During the struggle for existence, eunuchs suffer severe psychological stress and strain. They face identity crisis which makes them socially and psychologically insecure. To cope up with this abasement, eunuchs make many 'fake' relations in their pseudo-families for emotional security. This also supplements their feelings—to love and to be loved. In this identity crisis, eunuchs are forced to search for alternative sources for recognition.[3] Perhaps this is the most distinctive feature of politics of our times that various cultural groups demand political recognition and distinct identities. The groups making this demand have primarily been defined by their religion, their gender or their sexual orientation: Muslims, women or eunuchs for instance. The demand is that the democratic political system should open itself to these groups, should abandon policies that damage or ignore them and should strive to give them equal recognition alongside the mainstream cultural identities.

Thus the journey of endeavour for emancipation of the eunuch community will start with the removal of artificial barriers like prejudices about their physical and mental abilities, sexual handicappedness, social distance, etc. The journey has already started in a small way. In this journey, political recognition is not their sole motto, rather it is part of a strategy to get equal recognition in the society. For existence with pride and self-respect, eunuchs throughout India, especially, the ambitious ones are putting their efforts in getting themselves equipped and trained in various skills. Now-a-days, in Tamil Nadu, they prefer to be called as *aruvani* instead of *hijra* or *ali* and in order to become beauticians and therapists they are getting training from M. Nikkila, a famous beautician and therapist of Chennai.

They are making forays into the couture world also. Six eunuchs appeared as runway models in a fashion show (*Designer Passion*, 2000) held at Lucknow, the capital of U.P. in Northern India. They shared the stage with top models including the former miss India Gul Panag (*Hindustan Times*, New Delhi, 17 November 2000). A beauty contest for eunuchs 'Ms. World 2001' has also been organised at Bhopal, the capital of Madhya Pradesh during Holi, the festival of colours. More than 100 eunuchs competed in the contest (*Sunday Times*, 31 March 2002). In 2003, a eunuch fashion show was organised to mark the Holi celebration at Bhopal (*Times of India*, 19 March 2003). In Tamil Nadu, a very beautiful eunuch has been being selected as 'Miss Koovagam' every year during *Koovagam* festival.[4] To legitimise equal recognition, the eunuch community in Bangalore is organising *Hijra Habba*, a festival of sports and cultural events for eunuchs since 2002.

Generally, eunuchs are believed to have occult powers, so people invariably hand over their money whenever a group of eunuchs turn up at their house. Credit card companies, private banks, municipal corporations etc. exploited their 'this' power and employed them as recovery agents e.g. Patna Municipal Corporation gave a contract to the eunuchs for the collection of house tax in Patna city (*Dainik Bhaskar*, Gwalior, 9 September 2006). Eunuchs recovered money from delinquent customers. The recovery rate increased, unlike with musclemen who use power of fear, which can be dealt with, eunuchs use the power of embarrassment, which is much more difficult to tackle.

But these stingy jobs are insufficient to suffice their basic needs. At the same time, the traditional sources of income i.e., singing and dancing at auspicious occasions is drying up, as a result many eunuchs are coaxed into the world of prostitution to augment their income.[5] Soon it was realized by the eunuchs in the country that the struggle for existence is incomplete without their political emancipation. Virtually eunuchs have no safe space in the society not even in their native families from where they come. Their sexual identity has always been questioned and they are humiliated in all walks of life. The systematic violence that eunuchs face is reinforced by institutions like their families, educational institutions, hospitals, police, etc.

In this context, the cynical foul is evident in the legal system of the nineteenth century. The Criminal Tribes Act, 1871 was amended and made appropriate for eunuchs also in 1897 (An Act for the Registration of Criminal Tribes and Eunuchs). According to this Act, the local Government was required to keep a record of names and residences of all eunuchs who were suspected of kidnapping or castrating children or committing offences under Section 377 of the Indian Penal Code (IPC). The Act not only created mistrust for the eunuchs in the society but also strengthened the belief that eunuchs are child lifters. The law also deprives eunuchs from adopting any child, making a will, making a gift or being a guardian.

After living years on social periphery and under deprivation, eunuchs came forward for their welfare and to fight for socio-economic rights. They formed 'The All India Hijra Kalyan Sabha' on 4 November 1983. This Sabha demanded their civil rights from the Government as there is a provision of equal rights for every citizen of India under the Fundamental Rights of the Constitution of India. After a long struggle, the eunuchs were granted voting rights by the Supreme Court in 1986 (*The Telegraph*, 31 July 1994). Though eunuchs acquired all constitutional rights and are governed by laws that apply to all, the fact is that the eunuch community in India is still exerting to procure civil equality and basic human rights.

It is important to note that the lives of those children who are congenitally sexually incomplete are generally pathetic and miserable. From the family to the school and in the peer group these unfortunate children face lampoons, which in turn reflect in their schooling. 'The Eunuch Children Welfare Association' established in Bandel (West Bengal) is striving for the education of the sexually handicapped children. These children either do not get admission in the school or have to leave due to humiliation and embarrassment. Similarly, 'National Association of Nar-Naris of India' (NANNI) of Mumbai aims to work for the education and employment of eunuchs. Therefore, many NGOs and Welfare Organisations throughout the country raised their voice against various social discrepancies and bigotry. After enfranchisement, it was just like floodgates opened for the eunuchs and could be considered as the first step towards their political recognition.

Santosh of Bhuchho Mandi (dist. Bhatinda, Punjab) was the first eunuch to win the election in the democratic India in 1992. After this victory, many eunuchs chose the path of politics for their political emancipation. But this victory was not enough to gain mainstream respect. Even the basics of bureaucracy posed challenges. One of the first stumbling blocks was the election nomination papers which offers only two sex options. Shobha Nehru, Kamala Jaan, Shabnam Mausi, Heera Bai etc. all these eunuch politicians contested their elections as woman candidates and not with their existing sexual status of 'eunuch' or 'third gender'. After every election, eunuch contestant has to face allegation of misleading declaration of the sexual status.

The consequent victories of eunuchs in the elections on the one hand raised their morale but at the same time it ruffled the mainstream politics. The success of Kamala Jaan as Mayor of Katni (M.P.) was first regarded as accidental and then the achievement of Shabnam Mausi as first M.L.A. as a coincidence. These victories of eunuchs especially in Madhya Pradesh compelled to meditate on the issue. Analysts viewed their emergence as a growing indication of people's disillusionment with the political class and labelled political eunuchs as eunuch local politicians.

National political parties argued that national or state level issues are irrelevant in local body elections and that could be the reason for them losing the election. According to Arjun Singh, ex-Chief Minister of M.P., the victory of eunuchs in election is a symbol of democratic maturity, a lesson to the representatives (*Navbharat*, 19 September 2002). Digvijay Singh, then Chief Minister of M.P. welcomed eunuchs into the active politics by saying "the victory of eunuchs is due to their political awareness and enthusiasm in this field" (*Dainik Bhaskar*, 1 February 2000). Uma Bharti, former leader of Bhartiya Janata Party, on the election of Shabnam Mausi, criticized people for showing disrespect to a eunuch. She said, "It is really sad that we are not giving a person his/her due respect in the society. Like others eunuchs also have the right to live in this society with respect and dignity. We should change our attitude towards them." (*PTI*, 27 February 2000).

In brief, the election of eunuchs brought forward two types of reactions: first type of reaction was similar to the opinion of M.S. Gill, former Chief Election Commissioner. He inferred that, "this is a no-confidence feeling towards our political representatives. Accordingly, this has opened the doors for the active participation of eunuchs in democratic process. As a result, eunuchs will come out of the social rejection and on the other hand this phenomenon will be a lesson to political parties." The second type of reaction was in contrast with the above. Shrinivas Tiwari, the former speaker of M.P. Assembly has questioned the credentials of eunuchs in democratic process and warned that if the demolition of political values continues like this, democracy will be eunuchised (*Dainik Bhaskar*, 6 March 2000).

Analysis of all these viewpoints indicates that the victory of eunuchs was an indication of electorates' disenchantment with corrupt politicians. They voted to snub the political parties and were sceptical of how effective eunuchs will be in politics, as has generally been said. The fact is, it was a case of pulling somebody up and once that happens, they get visibility.[6] Eunuchs themselves know that if they enter the public domain of electoral politics, governmental power will lead to their recognition. Therefore, the victory of eunuchs in elections could be considered a marked step towards social acceptance for a community that has been reviled for centuries and can be regarded as their commitment and conviction with the public.

Moreover, we find that their slogans were carefully coined, keeping in mind that they cannot deliver long charismatic speeches to influence public. Hence, in the framework of few sentences, they carved their self-assertion and confidence like:

> *'Kinnar ko jetao, vanshwad se chhutkara pao'*
> (Choose a eunuch, get rid off nepotism).
>
> *'Nikamme netaon ka ek ilaj,*
> *hijron ke sar par rakh do taj'*
> (Teach the worthless politicians a lesson, put the crown on the head of the eunuch).
>
> *'Rajniti ling se nahin, dimag aur imandari se ki jaati hai'*
> (You don't need genitals for politics, you need brain and integrity).
>
> *'Kunwaron ko lao, Bharat bachao'*
> (It's time for bachelors to save India)

All these slogans had hidden messages for the public which provoked them against nepotism, corruption etc., warned them for torpiel politicians, showed their determination and gave impetus to choose eunuchs as alternative candidates.

Subsequent success stories of eunuchs compelled the think tanks of the political parties to become optimistic and offered them the membership. In the year 2000, many eunuchs joined political parties in Madhya Pradesh,[7] but they never got ticket even for the post of councillor/corporator. Consequently, most of the disheartened eunuchs left the parties.

On April 5, 2000 eunuchs of M.P. united for the first time to make *Jan Vikas Kinnar Front,* patronaged by Kamala Jaan of Katni and Shabnam Mausi of Sohagpur for the welfare and development of society (*Dainik Bhaskar,* 6 April 2000). Unfortunately, this front could not fulfil their aspirations. Hence, in 2003 they formed a political party 'Jeeti Jitai Party' (J.J.P.). Nearly 20 eunuchs contested the M.P. State Assembly Election 2003 under this party banner and all the contestants lost the ballot field. Analysts and psephologists said the battle of eunuchs is over. Their charisma will not repeat in future.

On careful analysis of the election results, it can be interpreted that the victory of B.J.P. in the state came through the *Hindutva Card* while the eunuchs in Madhya Pradesh are mostly Muslims, so the eunuch lost to polarised votes.

In this journey for political emancipation, they begot many role-models like Kamala Jaan, Shabnam Mausi, Heera Bai, Gulshan, etc. All these role models managed to have public recognition at the same time are still to win legitimacy for the third sex.

After Kamala Jaan controversy, eunuchs became much more alert in revealing their sexual identity. Since then no such dispute has surfaced. Analysts are claiming that success of eunuchs in electoral politics was merely a coincidence on the one hand, on the other eunuchs claim to rule India one day.

## Notes

1. Neither eunuchs could inherit property, nor could they marry. They were considered even lower than *sudras* among Hindus and among Muslims they had to stand behind men and women while offering *namaz*.
2. It will be appropriate to bring about the distinction between authority and leadership. Authority means the right to control, attached to the *gaddi* (office), involving respect, submission and reverence shown towards those who represent the office or who are invested with its rights. Here, we are not concerned with the authority of an individual or a group, but are concerned with the authority derived due to his/her post or position.
3. I am calling it politics of the mainstream because in the democratic country like India, eunuchs should have right to live like other groups without any discrimination on the basis of their sexual status. Many educated eunuchs do not get jobs merely due to their ambiguous sex. Even the census of India have asked eunuchs to enrol themselves as male or female as per their wish but are not recognised as they are i.e., eunuch or third gender.
4. This festive occasion or marriage ceremony of eunuchs with the deity warrior 'Aravan' becomes an important news item every year. In Southern India, eunuchs consider themselves as the descendants of Lord Krishna. Every year, on the full moon day, by the end of April, eunuchs get married. Their marriage is solemnised at *Koovagam*, a

village in Tamil Nadu, where thousands of eunuchs gather from all over the country to celebrate the festival. Dressed in bridal attire, they go to the temple of 'Aravan' who they call *Koothandavar* and wed the deity. According to Hindu mythology, Aravan is the son of Arjuna, the central character of the epic *Mahabharata*. To ensure victory of Arjuna, Aravan had to be sacrificed to God. He was chosen for being the most perfect of men. But Aravan had one wish, he asked to get married and enjoy sexual bliss on his last night alive. No woman, however, would consent to marry a man hours away from his death and in the end Lord Krishna transformed himself into a woman and became his bride 'Mohini'. Next day, Krishna performed the rituals of a 'widow'.

This ceremony became a tradition for eunuchs, who every year come out of their ghetto and perform an age-old ritual. They assemble in the temple's courtyard, in front of the idol, priest tie the sacred red thread around their neck chanting the *mantras* and they revel in it. On the following morning eunuchs beat their chests in grief on having been widowed.

5. According to a newspaper, nearly two-third eunuchs are believed to be working as prostitutes (*The Weekend Observer*, New Delhi, 23 October 1993). Basically, eunuchs are sodomites and have one or more sexually transmitted diseases (STD) and many of them are HIV positive. A study of the eunuchs in Bombay by Dr. Gilada of the Indian Health Organisation which started in 1989 revealed 11 per cen of the eunuch population tested HIV positive. In 1992, he found 40 per cent of the eunuch prostitutes to be infected with AIDS (*Hindustan Times*, New Delhi, 14 March 1994).

   Many NGOs and Welfare Organisations, social activists, doctors and even AIDS control cell of the Government of India are active in protecting eunuchs from AIDS. NAZ Foundation India Trust, Dai Welfare Society, Dr. I.S. Gilada, etc. are working on HIV and sexual health. They educate eunuchs in this regard through awareness programmes, workshops, free distribution of condoms, etc.
6. Zia Jaffrey (1996) in her book *The invisibles: A Tale of the Eunuchs of India* (New York: Pantheon Books) inclines to view that eunuchs may reasonably be described as the invisibles.
7. During interviews, it has been found that Bano Jaan of Rewa along with her *chelas* (disciples) is member of Bhartiya Janta Party (BJP) Shanti Bai of Dhamanka, Gwalior is member of Congress (I). According to the newspaper, on 31 March 2000, 20 eunuchs of Lashkar (West) constituency and a few from Lashkar (East) joined BJP (*Dainik Bhaskar*, 16 April 2003).
8. It is worthwhile to mention that in passport, eunuchs managed to have another option besides male/female i.e. 'E' or Eunuch.

# FIVE

# Demographic Profile of Eunuchs

In order to study the political behaviour of eunuchs, standard approach has been adopted to determine what influences their basic orientations toward politics and their participation in different political activities. It is believed that independent variables (the personal information of the respondents and particulars about the families they come from) shape political behaviour.

The survey covered six districts of Madhya Pradesh to draw a representative sample. These districts were selected on the basis of the concentration of eunuchs who had contested elections so far or the region of their influence. The total number of eunuchs interviewed was 53—consisting of eunuchs who had contested elections and those who had not or aspired to contest. 13 are from Bhopal district, 12 from Jabalpur, 9 from Gwalior, 8 from Guna, 7 from Rewa and 4 from Shahdol district.

Table 5.1 gives the information of eunuchs who had contested elections for different posts in Madhya Pradesh. This information is primarily based on our investigations and on the newspaper clippings.

Table 5.2 reveals that out of 53 respondents surveyed, maximum eunuchs (62.26%) were of 18-35 years of age, and 8 eunuchs (15.09%) were of 51-65 years of age, while 6 eunuchs (11.32%) were in the age-group of 36-50 years and the same numbers of eunuchs were over 65 years of age.

**Table 5.1:** Eunuchs who had contested elections in Madhya Pradesh

| No. | *Name of the candidate* | *Constituency* | *Election year* | *Post* | *Result* |
|---|---|---|---|---|---|
| 1. | Kamala Jaan | Katni | 1999 | Mayor | won |
| | | Mudwara | 2003 | MLA | defeated |
| 2. | Heera Bai | Jabalpur | 2000 | Corporator | won |
| | | Jabalpur (Central) | 2000 | MLA | defeated |
| 3. | Meena Bai | Sehora Dist. Jabalpur | 2000 | Chairperson Municipal Committee | won |
| 4. | Meena Bai | Sehora | 2003 | MLA | defeated |
| 5. | Suraiya | Bhopal (North) | 2003 | MLA | defeated |
| 6. | Rani Jaan (Payal) | American Ward, Sehore | 2000 | Corporator | won |
| | | Sehore | 2003 | MLA | defeated |
| 7. | Munna Raja | Ganj Basoda, Dist. Vidisha | 2003 | MLA | defeated |
| 8. | Gulshan | Veer Sawarkar Ward, Bina, Dist. Sagar | 2000 | Corporator | won |
| 9. | Panchi Deshmukh | Itarsi, Dist. Hoshangabad | 2003 | MLA | defeated |
| 10. | Shabnam Mausi | Sohagpur, Dist. Sehdol | 2000 | MLA | won |
| | | | 2003 | MLA | defeated |
| | | Kotma, Dist. Anuppur | 2008 | MLA | defeated |
| 11. | Bano Jaan | Rewa | 2003 | MLA | defeated |
| 12. | Maya Bai | Satna | 2004 | Corporator | defeated |
| 13. | Reshma | Chhatarpur | 2003 | MLA | defeated |
| 14. | Pooja Bai | Chachauda, Dist. Guna | 2003 | MLA | defeated |
| 15. | Champa Nayak | Harda | 2000 | Chairperson Municipal Committee | defeated |
| 16. | Shanti Bai Khatik | Vill. Dhamanka, Teh.Dabra, Dist. Gwalior | 2000 | Sarpanch | won |
| | | Dabra, Dist. Gwalior | 2010 | Member Janpad | defeated |
| 17. | Kamala Bua | Sagar | 2009 | Mayor | won |
| 18. | Lali Bai (Kinnar) | Shivpuri | 2008 | MLA | defeated |

*Source:* Information Based on personal interviews with the eunuchs and related newspaper clippings.

**Table 5.2:** Distribution of respondents according to their age

| *Age-group (in years)* | *No. of eunuchs (N-53)* | *Percentage* |
|---|---|---|
| 18 – 35 | 33 | 62.26 |
| 36 – 50 | 6 | 11.32 |
| 51 – 65 | 8 | 15.09 |
| Above 65 | 6 | 11.32 |

It is noteworthy that the younger eunuchs are the main earners of the community, therefore, the age-group of 18-35 years are ever expanding. The *akhadas* having younger eunuchs are considered to be the rich and the powerful. The good looking young eunuchs are called *'naginas'* and are always in demand for auction. Hence, the number of eunuchs at one *akhada* is not fixed and most of them do not remain permanently at their original point of entry into the community.

**Table 5.3:** Distribution of respondents according to their religion/caste before joining the community

| *Religion/Caste* | *No. of eunuchs (N-53)* |
|---|---|
| Hindu | 27 |
| (i) Brahmin | 8 |
| (ii) Kshatriya | 3 |
| (iii) Vaishya | — |
| (iv) Scheduled caste | 9 |
| (v) Backward class | 7 |
| Muslim | 16 |
| Sikh | — |
| Christian | — |
| Scheduled tribe | 7 |
| Don't know | 3 |

When eunuchs were classified on the basis of their religion/caste before joining the community, it was found that the eunuchs represent almost all the known religions/caste except Vaishya (Hindu), Sikh and Christian. 27 out of 53 were Hindus, 16 Muslims and 7 Scheduled Tribes before joining the eunuch community, whereas, the rest 4 reported that they didn't know about their family background as they were too young at the time of joining the eunuch community.

Castewise distribution of the respondents shows that 8 eunuchs belonged to brahmin families, 9 to scheduled caste, 7 to backward class and 3 to kshatriya. But after joining the eunuch community the whole lifestyle of the individual changes, irrespective of his previous religion or caste.

**Table 5.4:** Religion followed by the respondents at present

| *Religion* | *No. of eunuchs (N-53)* | *Percentage* |
|---|---|---|
| Hindu | 12 | 22.64 |
| Muslim | 37 | 69.81 |
| Both | 4 | 7.54 |

Table 5.4 gives information about the present religion of the respondents. 12 out of 53 (22.64%) reported that they are Hindus, nearly two third (37) claimed to be Muslims, while 4 eunuchs followed both the religions (Hindu as well as Muslim) impartially or they were syncretic.

Interestingly eunuchs may be either Hindus or Muslims, but all of them follow the Muslim rites and rituals for the dead persons' last rites. Throughout their life eunuchs either worship mother goddess or go to mosque but the fact is they have mixed influences of Hindu as well as Muslim customs and rituals on their behaviour and beliefs. Regardless of the fact whether a eunuch is Hindu or a Muslim the dead body is always buried in the Muslim tradition. They observe *Teeja, Chaaleeswa* and *Faatiha*. The Muslim inclination can be understood if one analyses the process of emasculation. During the course of the operation of castration, the neophyte is asked to cry out *'deen'* three times (This shows faith in Prophet Mohammad S.A.W.).

Sitara Nayak, a senior eunuch of Gwalior revealed that at present, all the *gaddis* of Madhya Pradesh are basically Muslims *gaddis* but the fact is that besides their present religious status all of them worship Bahuchara Mata. They have photographs of the goddess in their *ala* (shelf). They are also seen partaking in the important Hindu festivals like *Navaratri, Gangaur, Dussera, Diwali, Holi,* etc.

**Table 5.5:** Distribution of respondents according to their educational level

| *Education level* | *No. of eunuchs (N-53)* | *Percentage* |
|---|---|---|
| Illiterate | 38 | 71.69 |
| Primary | 8 | 15.09 |
| Middle | 4 | 7.54 |
| Secondary | 3 | 5.66 |

Table 5.5 shows that out of 53 eunuchs surveyed, 38 (71.69%) were illiterate. Some of them were either school drop-outs or had no education. 8 respondents had received school education upto the primary level, 4 passed middle and only 3 passed their secondary level.

The respondents, who had proceeded beyond primary level of education narrated that they had faced difficulties in school as they were discriminated against, were subjected to the sarcastic comments of the teachers and the classmates about their ambiguous genitalia. All these made them hopeless and helpless to continue their studies.

**Table 5.6:** Occupation of the biological father of respondents

| *Occupation* | *No. of eunuchs (N-53)* | *Percentage* |
|---|---|---|
| Farmer | 23 | 43.39 |
| Labour | 10 | 18.86 |
| Artisan | 6 | 11.32 |
| Small Business (shopkeeper) | 5 | 9.43 |
| Govt. Service (Lower grade) | 7 | 13.20 |
| Govt. Service (Upper grade) | 1 | 1.88 |
| Landlord | 1 | 1.88 |

Table 5.6 depicts that majority of respondents came from families of farmers and labourers (33 out of 53). There were 12 others whose biological fathers were small businessmen (shop-keepers) or lower grade Government servants such as peons, drivers, carpenters, etc., whereas 1 eunuch belonged to the

family of a landlord and the same number to the family of a Government Officer.

**Table 5.7:** Educational level of the biological parents of respondents

| *Educational level* | *Father (N-53)* | *Percentage* | *Mother (N-53)* | *Percentage* |
|---|---|---|---|---|
| Illiterate | 29 | 54.71 | 41 | 77.35 |
| Primary | 9 | 16.98 | 9 | 16.98 |
| Middle | 7 | 13.20 | 2 | 3.77 |
| Secondary | 4 | 7.54 | — | — |
| Graduate | 3 | 5.66 | — | — |
| Post-Graduate | 1 | 1.88 | 1 | 1.88 |

The data for educational level of biological parents of the respondents shows that majority of the eunuchs surveyed belonged to the illiterate families. In case of father, 29 (54.71%) were illiterate, 9 (16.98%) primary, 7 (13.20%) middle, 4 (7.54%) secondary, 3 (5.66%) graduate and only 1 (1.88%) post-graduate. And no mother was found to have secondary or graduate and 9 (16.98%) had primary, 2 (3.77%) middle and only 1 (1.88%) post-graduate, whereas 41 (77.35%) constituted to be illiterate.

In this chapter an attempt has been made to assess the impact of selected social factors on the political orientation of eunuchs. These factors include the background of their natal families as well as their socio-economic status in the eunuch community. Some eunuchs failed to provide the information regarding the natal families due to two wrinkles: first, they were too young at the time of joining the community or after castration they were precluded to have any affiliation with their natal families. Information regarding their income appeared to be fabricated and misleading. Their income was quite contradictory with the amenities they had in *akhadas* and the life they lead.

Therefore, the eunuchs had to provide information related to two families, one where they were born and the other, where they were nourished and socialised with pseudo family bondings. The genes inherited are nurtured by the community which has atypical norms, rites and rituals. And also their age of recruitment varies from infant to adulthood. Hence, there is hardly any influence of socio-economic status of natal families on their behaviour rather it is their socialisation by the community which impinge their behaviour at large.

Although, the socio-economic status of the natal families have nothing to do with their present behaviour, their present socio-economic status definitely manifest in their political orientation and participation. The SES model given by Verba, Nie and Kim (1978) rightly states that the higher the socio-economic status, the more the person is likely to feel that he/she can influence politics (efficacy), the greater the political interest, the more the sense of civil duty. These, in turn, increase the likelihood of political participation. In the course of survey, we noticed that eunuchs who were affluent enough or were *nayaks* like Shabnam Mausi, Kamala Jaan, Heera Bai, Suraiya, etc. contested elections either for local, mayoral or MLA, therefore, it can be recapitulated that those eunuchs who had satisfied their basic human needs, strived for self-esteem and self-actualization.

# Six
# Political Consciousness in Eunuchs

In the previous chapter we discussed the independent variables elucidated in Section-I of the main interview-schedule. Section-II, III and IV deal with dependent variables of political behaviour i.e. political consciousness, political participation and value orientation of eunuchs which are analysed in the present and the following chapters.

The present chapter analyses political consciousness—an integral part of the political behaviour of eunuchs—which includes the interest shown by them in political matters and their knowledge and awareness of political events occurring inside and outside the nation and a willingness to participate in it.

In order to assess the political consciousness among eunuchs, a scale of 10 questions has been constructed which covers their knowledge of political parties, awareness of political rights, their interest and willingness to participate in the political events, etc. The collected data were classified question-wise and to get a complete picture of the variable, weightages were given to the answers of the respondents. Only main questions were scored and sub-questions were analysed and interpreted. A score of 1 was given to positive responses i.e. 'yes' and 0 to negative ones i.e. 'No'. The score for all questions were summed up and a composite score for political consciousness for each of the fifty-three eunuchs were worked out (shown in Table 6.8). The scores for political consciousness of the eunuchs varied between 0-15.

**Table 6.1:** Responses of respondents regarding casting of vote

| *Responses* | *No. of eunuchs (N-53)* | *Percentage* |
|---|---|---|
| Always | 42 | 79.24 |
| Sometimes | 4 | 7.54 |
| Never | 7 | 13.20 |

As regard to the interest of respondents in casting vote in parliamentary, assembly or corporation/panchayat elections, it was found that 79.24 per cent (42 out of 53) eunuchs always exercised their franchise right, 7.54 per cent (4) responded that they voted sometimes, whereas 13.20 (7) never casted their vote.

As a matter of fact, for a very long time, the existence of eunuchs as a community was not recognised by the law of the land. Their urge to be part of the mainstream of society, and to have the right to vote in their own chosen identity, had been growing in the community. After a long struggle, the eunuchs were granted voting rights by the Supreme Court of India in 1986. This led to the Election Commission's direction to include eunuchs on the electoral rolls. The then Chief Election Commissioner T.N. Seshan had left it to the eunuchs to decide whether they wanted their names registered in the voter's list as male or female (*Indian Express*, 3 November 1994; *Times of India*, 6 November 1994). Ironically they have never been banned, but most were overlooked in counting, unless they had registered as 'male' in the census form, often against their wishes.

Shabnam Mausi stated that in the past they used to vote along with female voters, but now-a-days, the polling booth officials ask them to vote without standing in a queue. Bano Jaan of Rewa who contested election for Municipal Corporation as BJP supported candidate said that the vote has become a new route to social recognition.

**Table 6.2:** Criteria on which respondents cast their votes

| *Responses* | *Criteria* | | | | | |
|---|---|---|---|---|---|---|
| | *Candidate* | | *Political Party* | | *Election* | *Campaign* |
| | *No.* | *%* | *No.* | *%* | *No.* | *%* |
| Yes | 22 | 41.50 | 38 | 71.70 | — | — |
| No | 31 | 58.50 | 15 | 28.30 | 53 | 100.00 |
| Total | 53 | 100.00 | 53 | 100.00 | 53 | 100.00 |

The respondents who participated in voting were asked the criteria of casting votes. Out of the total respondents, 71.70 per cent attributed the criteria to the political party and 41.50 per cent considered the image of the candidate.

It has been observed that voting on the basis of the image of a political party was quite a stereotypical response. As a matter of fact, in an *akhada* the viewpoint of the *guru* motivates the perspectives of all its members. Most of them are blind followers of their *guru*, therefore, electoral campaigns do not affect them at all. But the figures show that in some cases credentials of the candidates do influence voting.

**Table 6.3:** Responses of respondents regarding the party preference

| *Responses* | *No. of eunuchs (N-53)* | *Percentage* |
|---|---|---|
| Yes | 45 | 84.90 |
| No | 8 | 15.10 |

If *'yes'* then, the name of the political party

(i) Congress (I) 40
(ii) Bhartiya Janta Party 5

The respondents were asked whether they were influenced by any particular political party or by its ideology in regard to voting. To this 84.90 per cent respondents said that they were influenced by a political party and preferred to vote for it, while 15.10 per cent responded that they did not prefer any political party.

The respondents were also asked to name the political party which motivated them to vote for it repeatedly, and it was found that 40 eunuchs were influenced by the Congress and considered it the oldest party of the country. Sitara Nayak of Gwalior emphasized that it is the party which fought for the independence, Shabnam Mausi preferred Congress because she considers Nehru and Indira Gandhi as ideal leaders. Being a member of Congress (I), Shanti Bai always voted for the party and similarly Bano Jaan and her four disciples of Rewa preferred BJP. On the contrary, Pooja of Binaganj, district Guna is amongst those eunuchs who do not prefer any political party, because she strongly feels that political parties do nothing for the public.

An enquiry about the oldest political party of India, major political parties of Madhya Pradesh and their regret after casting vote, elicited the information that most of the respondents knew the power of vote and after voting, they did not regret. They are cognizant about their rights, contemporary political parties in the state, and the oldest political party of India.

**Table 6.4:** Opinion of the respondents regarding joining politics

| *Opinion* | *No. of eunuchs (N-53)* | *Rank* |
|---|---|---|
| (i) For social service | 40 | I |
| (ii) To gain power and to make money | 16 | II |
| (iii) To uplift the social status | 11 | III |

Respondents were able to come up with the responses to the question 'Why should one join politics?'. This question produced a variety of responses. However, the above fit comfortably into the coding categories: for social service, to gain power and to make money and as a mean to uplift the social status.

Table 6.4 shows that the eunuchs placed high esteem (40) for social service. After that, there is fairly even support for the other coded categories i.e. to gain power (16) and to uplift their social status (11). What is worth observing is that the most common understanding of eunuchs to join politics is for social service or as functional, because they understand that they can get things done easily when they raise points about corruption and issues concerning the common man. The fair responses for joining politics to gain power and to uplift the social status indicate that eunuchs believe politics to be a marked step towards social recognition.

**Table 6.5:** Responses of respondents regarding collection of information related to politics

| *Responses* | *No. of eunuchs (N-53)* | *Percentage* |
|---|---|---|
| Yes | 47 | 88.68 |
| No | 6 | 11.32 |

If *'Yes'* then medium—

| *Medium* | *Frequency* | *Rank* |
|---|---|---|
| (i) Newspapers and Magazines | 9 | IV |
| (ii) Television/Radio | 38 | I |
| (iii) Telephone/Mobile phone | 21 | II |
| (iv) Personal contact | 16 | III |

For political orientation, an individual must have knowledge of the various political activities. Responding to the question whether they (eunuchs) gather information about local/national/international political events or are they oriented towards the larger political universe. In this regard, most of the eunuchs surveyed (88.68%) responded positively that they collected information related to politics from various sources.

There is no denying fact that the key agent of learning and moulding public opinion is the media. The mass media surround us and serve as a means of surveillance. The different means of mass media such as television, radio, newspapers, magazines, etc. can play a decisive role in arousing political awareness among the citizens, which in turn lead them to political participation and political development. When respondents were asked about the sources of gathering political information or their exposure to mass media, television was found to be the most effective and powerful medium of information. 38 out of 47 eunuchs were regular viewers and devoted their leisure time to television. Their talkative nature makes telephone and mobile phone the next most important source of information. Then comes the discussion and gossiping about the political affairs with friends and fellow eunuchs to further enhance and shape their political awareness. Being less literate, very few eunuchs (9 out of 47) gather information from the newspapers and magazines.

Inspired by the success of Kamala Jaan and Shabnam Mausi, eunuchs in Madhya Pradesh became politically active and posed a challenge in the key constituencies in 2003. Those eunuchs who stood in elections had to contest as independent candidates because no mainstream parties were willing to give them tickets. It has been found from the discussions with eunuchs that most of them were inclined towards certain ideologies of national parties. But soon they came out of the delusion, as sometimes they were not treated as they expected or they were not welcomed at all. Some of the aspirant eunuchs then decided to form a political party whose aims, ambitions, norms and even responsibilities were to be settled by themselves.

**Table 6.6:** Responses regarding the formation of a political party by eunuchs

| *Responses* | *No. of eunuchs (N-53)* | *Percentage* |
|---|---|---|
| Yes | 28 | 52.83 |
| No | 25 | 47.17 |

Table 6.6 reveals the responses regarding the formation of a political party [*Jeeti Jitai Party* (JJP)] by the eunuchs in Madhya Pradesh. Accordingly 52.83 per cent eunuchs surveyed justified the formation of a separate party of the eunuchs, for the eunuchs and by the eunuchs, whereas 47.17 per cent were not in its favour and they restricted themselves to the rights of casting votes only.

Suraiya Nayak, who contested election for the States' Assembly in 2003 from Bhopal (North) constituency and the founder member of JJP revealed that there were two motives behind the formation of separate political party—first, to unite the politically aspired and empathetic eunuchs on a single platform. Secondly, to project and promote the qualities of the community which show them differently from the rest of the world. The party was supposed to spread turf for the ambitious eunuch politicians and for making strategies for elections. The notions, that they had no family to harbour, they are honest and will prove to be better public servants' worked in their favour.

On the contrary, those eunuchs who disagreed with the formation of a party argued that politics is not their profession, it will not change their destiny and those who are enticed into politics should give up the community's profession. A senior eunuch of Bhopal said that the true eunuchs would flush out these phonies who are letting down their traditional profession for political ends.

**Table 6.7:** Responses regarding interest shown by the Government towards the welfare of the eunuch community

| *Responses* | *No. of eunuchs (N-53)* | *Percentage* |
|---|---|---|
| Yes | — | — |
| No | 53 | 100.00 |

It was surprising to find that all the eunuchs surveyed were disappointed with the attitude of the Government towards them. Though they were not focussed about their expectations they expected the Government to be much more responsive. Accordingly, Government should come forward to give opportunities to them to use their talent genuinely. Unlike male or female, no eunuch in the country is ever nominated to any seat or given any preference anywhere. They are barred from Government jobs, cannot bequeath their property and even insurance agencies refuse to insure their lives.

Illiteracy, insecurity, sterility, abasement, etc. are myriad factors which influence their responses. Their failures in life seem to be sublimated on the Government in spite of the fact that after independence, they had acquired nearly all the constitutional rights as any other citizen enjoys in the country.

**Table 6.8:** Political consciousness among eunuchs

| *Consciousness* | *No. of eunuchs (N-53)* | *Percentage* |
|---|---|---|
| 0 – 5 (Low) | 2 | 3.78 |
| 5 – 10 (Moderate) | 50 | 94.34 |
| 10 – 15 (High) | 1 | 1.88 |

The overall result indicates that by and large political consciousness among eunuchs under study is found to be moderate. Here, political consciousness is represented by a summed score of responses to 10 questions about their knowledge of political parties, awareness of political events, their interest and willingness to participate in the political activities, etc. The score for political consciousness for maximum (94.34%) eunuchs lies between 5 and 10 with a mean of 7.41, while the actual score for the scale ranges from 0-15.

The score so obtained is admittedly a crude indicator, but it is observed that after suffrage eunuchs got a new status as individuals who could enter the social as well as political domain. Encouraged by the success of some eunuchs, they had become politically aware and started using *janta ki sewa* kind of politically correct expressions and inclined to participate with more enthusiasm in politics.

# SEVEN
# Political Participation of Eunuchs and their Political Value

Generally, political participation denotes the involvement of an individual in the political system of a given society. It also implies peoples' actions which directly or indirectly influence governmental machinery. McClosky (1968) defines political participation as those voluntary activities by which members of a society share in the selection of rulers and directly or indirectly participate in the formation of public policy.

In the present study, political participation refers to the participation of eunuchs in political activities which include discussion of politics with friends, partisanship, electioneering for candidates, attending election meetings and casting of votes.

To examine the nature and extent of political participation of eunuchs, the data were collected by a scale of five questions (Section-III of main interview-schedule). The collected information was classified question-wise first and then to get a composite picture of the variable, weightages were given to the responses. A score of 1 was given to positive responses i.e., 'Yes' and 0 to negative ones i.e., 'No'. The aggregate score for political participation of the eunuchs ranges between 0–15.

Political participation is key dependent variable. Available literature on political participation suggests that participatory involvement by citizens can affect government decisions (Verba and Nie, 1972). To get a better sense of the manner by which eunuchs involve themselves and participate in politics, the Table 7.1 discussion the path of analysis was undertaken.

**Table 7.1:** Responses regarding discussions of political affairs with friends

| *Responses* | *No. of eunuchs (N-53)* | *Percentage* |
|---|---|---|
| Often | 6 | 11.32 |
| Sometimes | 17 | 32.08 |
| Never | 30 | 56.60 |

Eunuchs are fun loving people. After their *feras* (collection of alms) and domestic chores, they love chatting and gossiping. Table 7.1 shows that 56.60 per cent eunuchs under study do not discuss politics at all. Despite their negative responses we find that most of them do discuss politics. Somewhere in their minds they have the conflict on the political involvement—'whether eunuch should or should not'. On the one hand, they discuss the achievements of Shabnam Mausi, Kamala Jaan and other eunuchs who contested and won elections, and on the other, social prejudices toward them and their sheepish nature refrains them from getting involved in politics. 6 out of 53 eunuchs admitted that they often discuss political affairs with their fellow eunuchs and 17 discuss it occasionally but not always.

Interestingly, during the course of the study, it has been noted that prosperous eunuchs especially *gurus* express their feelings more openly and aspire to be in politics and want to become public figures, whereas poor and supine ones criticize the involvement of eunuchs in politics.

**Table 7.2:** Responses regarding the membership of the political party

| *Responses* | *No. of eunuchs (N-53)* | *Percentage* |
|---|---|---|
| Yes | 19 | 35.84 |
| No | 34 | 64.16 |

If *'yes'* then, name of the party and the period of their association—

| *Years of* association | *Political Parties* | | | |
|---|---|---|---|---|
| | *Congress* | *BJP* | *JJP* | *Others* |
| 0 - 5 | — | — | 13 | — |
| 5 - 10 | — | 4 | — | — |
| 10 - 15 | 1 | 1 | — | — |
| Total | 1 | 5 | 13 | — |

The success of eunuchs in local and state level elections in Madhya Pradesh as independent candidates was considered an indication of the electorates' resentment towards the politicians and politics. After their victory in elections, the political parties showed interest in them. But when parties came to action, eunuchs were thrown off-balance. They were not provided any space. Out of desperation eunuchs either left the parties and became independents or formed their own party Jeeti Jitai Party (JJP).

In the present study, 19 out of 53 eunuchs were members of different political parties, whereas 34 responded negatively. 13 were members of JJP, 5 of BJP and 1 of Congress (I).

Shanti Bai of village Dhamanka, district Gwalior is a

member of Congress (I) for more than 10 years. She contested and won election twice for village panchayat with the support of Congress party. Bano Jaan of Rewa is a member of BJP for more than 5 years and Suraiya and her disciples of Bhopal are of JJP.

Meena Bai of Sehora and Heera Bai of Jabalpur were elected for the post of Chairperson of Municipal Committee and Councillor respectively as independent candidates. They were courted by the Samajwadi Party for State Assembly Elections 2003, but party didn't help them in the election campaign, as a result they lost the election. Sooner their passion for the party weaned away.

However, many eunuchs like Meena Bai and Heera Bai, are still inclined towards national political parties. But due to persistent class/gender bias, are not members of any political party.

**Table 7.3:** Responses regarding participation in selected activities during elections, N-53

| *Responses* | *Selected activities* | | | | |
|---|---|---|---|---|---|
| | *Caste vote* | *Attend election meetings* | *Canvass* | *Read election material* | *Persuade others to vote* |
| Yes | 46<br>(86.79) | 30<br>(56.60) | 38<br>(71.70) | 31<br>(58.49) | 31<br>(58.49) |
| No | 7<br>(13.21) | 23<br>(43.40) | 15<br>(28.30) | 22<br>(41.51) | 22<br>(41.51) |

*Note*: Figures in parentheses indicate percentages.

Political participation not only includes discussion of political affairs with friends or joining a political party but it also includes participation of an individual directly or indirectly in the political system. In this context, respondents were queried about their political activities like casting of vote, attending election meetings, canvassing, reading election materials and persuading others to vote.

Table 7.3 shows the eunuchs themselves participating in all the selected five activities of elections. The casting of vote was the most preferred activity. 46 out of 53 eunuchs casted their votes in election, whereas 7 responded in the negation. Either they were below 18 years of age at the time of election or were unable to go to the polling booth due to their old age or sickness or they refused to vote because of derisive questions raised about their sexual identity.

56.60 per cent eunuchs attended election meetings, whereas 43.40 per cent said that they were not interested in the same. They considered it as fraudulent activity. However, being verbose, majority of them liked canvassing (71.70%) while 58.49 per cent liked persuading and motivating others through raising slogans, distributing pamphlets and the same percentage said that they kept election material and marked the activity of their choice. This response may not be true because only few literate eunuchs could read the material, rest of them just held banners and political symbols.

**Table 7.4:** Opinion regarding involvement of eunuchs in politics

| *Opinion* | *No. of eunuchs (N-53)* | *Percentage* |
|---|---|---|
| Good | 34 | 64.15 |
| Arguable | 11 | 20.76 |
| Not good | 8 | 15.09 |

When asked about their opinion regarding the involvement of eunuchs in politics, it was found that 64.15 per cent considered the eunuchs' participation in politics as good, 15.09 per cent were against their participation while 20.76 per cent thought it as arguable. The perceptions in this regard were assorted.

Shabnam Mausi considers politics as a mean of social service, Suraiya Nayak of Bhopal wants to rule the hearts of the people through her services. According to Sitara Nayak of Gwalior, vote empowers a person and bolsters to do social work. To Bano Jaan of Rewa, after disgracing parents, politics is one way to retrieve self-respect and social status in society. She regrets leaving the parental home and curses herself for letting down her parents. Now she thinks that her success in politics can bring back the honour and pride of her family. Puja of Binaganj, district Guna can retreat fellow eunuchs from singing and dancing and wants to work for their self-esteem.

At the same time, a few eunuchs were not in favour of the involvement of eunuchs in politics and considered it as an affront to the community. May be, it is due to the groupism within the community or due to the fear of losing the income through their traditional profession.

**Table 7.5:** List of methods by which eunuchs press their demands

| *Sl. No.* | *List of methods* | *No. of eunuchs (N-53)* | *Rank* |
|---|---|---|---|
| 1. | Hunger strike | 18 | III |
| 2. | Gherao | 20 | II |
| 3. | Brick bats | 5 | V |
| 4. | Processions and demonstrations | 6 | IV |
| 5. | Peaceful negotiations | 48 | I |

Looking at the responses regarding the methods eunuchs applied to press their demands, it was found that they adopted more than one method. They wanted to achieve their demands by hook or crook. The responses so gathered were also rated according to the most preferred way to the least preferred one. Majority of the eunuchs advocated peaceful talks with elected representatives and public officials to get the work done and if it failed, they would try some other methods to press their demands. The second most common method was *gherao*. Actually *gherao* is a violent method but here it becomes more assertive when accompanied with their typical clapping. The next method, eunuchs preferred was hunger strike which unfortunately has not been practised so far especially by their community in Madhya Pradesh. According to them processions, demonstrations and brick batting were the least opted methods to press the demands.

It is observed that the behaviour of eunuchs is generally sexually suggestive which they knowingly show to perturb individuals, if their demands are not fulfilled, they become outrageous and in some cases they even take off their clothes to reveal exactly what physical anomaly lies underneath their clothes. This behaviour adds fear and revulsion in individuals and they try to get rid of them.

**Table 7.6:** Political participation of eunuchs

| *Political participation* | *No. of eunuchs (N-53)* | *Percentage* |
|---|---|---|
| 0 – 5 (Low) | 21 | 39.62 |
| 5 – 10 (Moderate) | 16 | 30.19 |
| 10 – 15 (High) | 16 | 30.19 |

This chapter begins by examining the political participation of eunuchs with their discussions on political matters, membership of the political parties, participation in various political activities, views regarding political involvement and their pressure tactics to get the work done. The above Table 7.6 displays the overall political participation of eunuchs under study. The data shows that nearly 40.0 per cent eunuchs were less politically active and 60.0 per cent were either highly active or moderately active. Most of the eunuchs' activities (political) were restricted to voting, canvassing and persuading others to vote. But as far as their self-indulgence was concerned, most of them were found to be cynical. By and large, majority of them were happy with the accomplishment of a few eunuchs, but some disheartened eunuchs neither liked to discuss political affairs nor appreciated participation of their community members in politics, hence, the latter exhibited low political participation. However, political discussions within the *akhada* definitely affect their orientation toward politics from *gurus* to *chelas* or from *chelas* to *chelas,* which in turn enhances their political participation.

In the paragraphs to come, a representative argument for the value orientation of eunuchs is analysed and summarised.

## Value Orientation of Eunuchs

The term value is generally employed to designate a dominant interest, motive or broad evaluative attitude. In this section of the interview-schedule (Section-IV) an attempt has been made to discover and compare values of eunuchs, especially political value in comparison with other values (theoretical, economic, aesthetic, social and religious). For a quick and superficial comparison of values of each of the 53 eunuchs, a scale of six representative questions with four alternative statements has been constructed on the basis of the Spranger's six value scale. These four alternatives were rated in order of their personal preferences, giving 4 to the most preferred statement, 3 to the second most preferred, 2 to the next one and 1 to the least preferred statement. The average of the scale thus remained the same at 16 for each value. The average score below 8 was considered low and above 8, high.

The values of each eunuch were assessed and compared with each other by ranking the six values from the highest to the lowest on the basis of average scores. The relative positions of the different values thus obtained are mentioned in the Table 7.7.

**Table 7.7:** Value orientation of Eunuchs, N-53

| *Sl. No.* | *Values* | *Average score* | *Rank* |
|---|---|---|---|
| 1. | Theoretical | 7.75 | V |
| 2. | Economic | 8.64 | III |
| 3. | Aesthetic | 7.64 | VI |
| 4. | Social | 10.01 | I |
| 5. | Political | 8.58 | IV |
| 6. | Religious | 9.30 | II |

Table 7.7 reveals that eunuchs attached the highest importance to social value, indicating that they appreciate 'love of people'. Their interest in people seems natural because they do not take binding relationship very seriously. The only people they love are other eunuchs and the public that nurture them. Normally, it has been observed that eunuchs show the philanthropic aspect of love and try to maintain good relationship with neighbours, they adopt poor children and occasionally bear marriage expenses of poor girls. Although people satirize them, eunuchs take it casually and reciprocate with sexually charged jokes and try to maintain concord.

The ranking of religious value in the second place, show the eunuchs' firm desire to comprehend the cosmos and to see the unity of people with the cosmic totality. Though eunuchs' chief deity is Bahuchara Mata in Gujarat, the eunuchs of Madhya Pradesh show their main affiliations to Islam and are seen visiting places sacred to Muslims. They visit Ajmer Shareef as it is a holy place for them. And at Ajmer there is a tomb of a eunuch at Tara hill. It is believed that this eunuch was blessed by the Khwaja Sahib. They say that the biggest religious event in their life is the *Haj*. They acquire respectful status after performing *Haj*, become *Hajis* and stop doing *feras*. However, the third most preferred value is economic value. To live in this materialistic world they adopt practical approach to satisfy their physical needs and embrace all possible ways like singing, dancing, prostitution etc. to earn money.

Next, the relatively high esteem given to political value indicates that after becoming financially well placed, eunuchs are interested in power and prestige. Being marginalised, income will always remain their priority, hence ranked political value as fourth (after economic value). The lowest value assessment for the theoretical and aesthetic approach as fifth and sixth ranks respectively, probably indicates that they are least interested in cognitive approaches to things. Their clothes, getup and even their lifestyle have no harmony and artistic outlook.

Thus, the present study reveals that the eunuchs showed high social, religious, economic and political values but low theoretical and aesthetic values. The findings so generated, confers the study of Kumar (1964) which reports that higher social, economic and political values and low theoretical value indicates leadership quality. Hence, it can be inferred that eunuchs have leadership quality and it can flourish if optimistic circumstances are provided.

# EIGHT

# Summing up the Political Behaviour of Eunuchs

Eunuchs have always been part of the Indian society albeit in a marginal way. As long as they were restricted to their traditional activities of singing and dancing at weddings, blessing newborn or taking part in such ceremonies, they were not even discussed. But the moment they started becoming an integral part of this heterogeneous society, by taking part and even winning elections, people started discussing and defining them from various angles according to each one's viewpoints and outlook. Now eunuchs are not a segment of the news—they are the 'news'.

After the victory of Kamala Jaan, besides not saluting the public verdict, the one who lost the battle challenged her sexual status. Though, the court acknowledged their psyche, but ultimately recognized and defined the biological point of view and ruled that eunuchs are technically male, subsequently barring them from seeking elected offices reserved for women. As per this ruling Kamala Jaan had to leave the post before the completion of her tenure due to sexual ambiguity. (The judgement of the Additional District Judge, Katni disqualified her from the post of Mayor in Katni Municipal Corporation on August 29, 2002 on the basis of gender).

Leaders of different political parties evaded making any comments on the entry of eunuchs into politics and only superficially welcomed them. At the same time analysts were

1. A eunuch going for *'fera'* (Visit)

2. Eunuchs singing and dancing on an auspicious occasion

3. A group of eunuchs blessing a new born baby

4A. Unique Paradox: Eunuchs follow Hindu as well as Muslim

4B. Unique Paradox: Eunuchs follow Hindu as well as Muslim religions

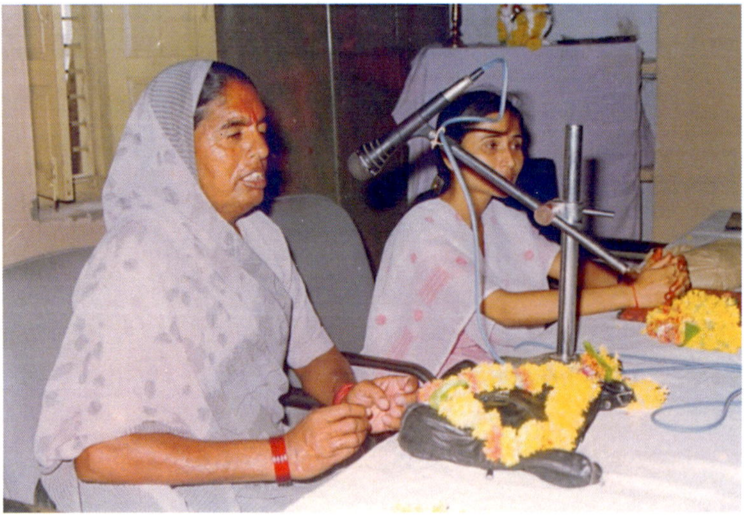

5. Shanti Bai Khatik, Sarpanch of Dhamanka, Dabra, Gwalior addressing a public meeting

6. Three eunuchs wishing for the victory of their *Guru*

7. Kamala Jaan (Mayor of Katni) as a Chief Guest in a *'Holi'* Festival at Gwalior

8. Shabnam Mausi, the former MLA with her *Chela* (Disciple)

9. Stylish eunuch *guru* Suraiya contested from Bhopal North in 2003 for the post of MLA

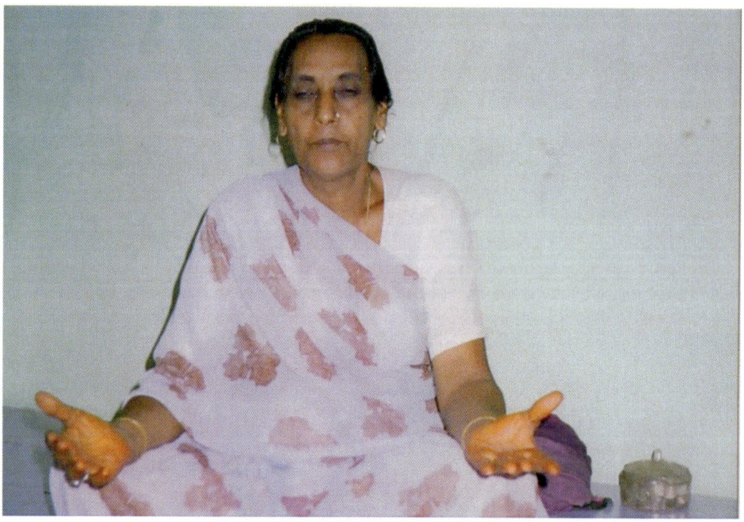

10. Meena Bai of Sehora narrating the success story of her election

11. Pooja Bai of Binaganj with her clan during an election campaign

12. Lali Bai (Kinnar) of Shivpuri during one of her election campaigns in the general elections 2008

13. Kamala Bua after being elected as Mayor of Sagar

unanimous in what they called "their victory by chance or an unrepeatable happening" and predicted that they have no future in politics.

Encouraged by the victory of Kamala Jaan, eunuchs in Madhya Pradesh started lining-up for politics and got success, their political behaviour muffled some critics on one hand and on the other, provoked thousands of questions in the minds of the curious. The design of the present study is an outcome of those unsolved questions. Generally, eunuchs are labelled with anomie views, considered cynical and less likely to be politically involved. But eunuchs believed they can tilt the scales in elections. When they raised points about corruption and issues concerning the common man they got instant applause from the public.

Now, the question is not whether eunuchs should have voting rights or not, the decision has already been taken in this regard. Here, the question is whether in a democratic country like India, where every citizen has voting rights, is it necessary to categorise the sexual identity in the conventional Male/Female category? Why cannot they be accepted 'as they are'. Does efficiency and calibre depend on sexual identity? If the answer is 'yes', it in turn will cast aspirations on the integrity of eunuch politicians, like Shabnam Mausi, Hira Bai, Gulshan, Meena Bai, etc. who have completed their tenure without any controversy. Their success in civil-polls as well as in Assembly election during 1999-2003 in Madhya Pradesh stimulated me to take up this study with some objectives which I thought was important to analyse. The objectives are analysed on the basis of factual informations gathered through interview-schedules and observations, and are summed up in Tables 8.1. By using eclectic approach it is not intended to give the impression that any single factor is independent, rather to make it clear that various factors like social, psychological as well as economic factors operate in the complex interaction in their behaviour. Therefore, many variables are juxtaposed to find out the reasons and circumstances that led eunuchs to join politics and also to assess their present situation.

**Table 8.1:** Relationship between political consciousness and political participation of the eunuchs, N–53

| Political consciousness | Political participation | | |
|---|---|---|---|
| | Low (0–5) | Moderate (5–10) | High (10–15) |
| (0–5) Low | 1 | 1 | — |
| (5–10) Moderate | 20 | 15 | 15 |
| (10–15) High | — | — | 1 |

While comparing political consciousness and political participation of eunuchs, it has been found that there is no significant difference between the above two ($\chi^2 = 3.23$; df 4; $p > 0.01$). It is clear from the above data that the political participation is not much influenced by political awareness. Table 8.1 shows moderate political awareness, the awareness which they acquire generally through interaction with people and consorts. The political awareness was instrumental in just motivating eunuchs to cast their votes sincerely. A few successes in politics were not enough to raise the self-confidence, political interest and involvement of eunuchs.

When eunuchs are taken seriously and considered capable of doing a better job of governing, efficacy in them will enhance on both personal as well as social front. On personal front, eunuchs will get recognition and opportunity to prove their worthiness to the society, whereas, the success of eunuchs in politics will encourage other members of the community to join them. Hence, it will influence both participation and awareness or *vice-versa*. The present data shows that the handful success of eunuchs has failed to stimulate the eunuch community, apart from moderate awareness. Even after this the political participation has been minimum.

It is very interesting to compare all three dependent variables considered in the study to analyse political behaviour of eunuchs. Table 8.2 depicts how far political value influence political consciousness and political participation. Surprisingly it has been found that the political value of the eunuchs' personality did not make any significant difference on political consciousness and political participation.

**Table 8.2:** Political value, political consciousness and political participation of the eunuchs, N–53

| *Political value* | *Political consciousness* | | | *Political participation* | | |
|---|---|---|---|---|---|---|
| | *Low (0–5)* | *Moderate (5–10)* | *High (10–15)* | *Low (0–5)* | *Moderate (5–10)* | *High (10–15)* |
| Low (0–8) | 2 | 22 | — | 11 | 10 | 3 |
| High (8–16) | — | 28 | 1 | 10 | 6 | 13 |
| $\chi^2$ | | 3.26 | | | 6.87 | |
| Significance at 0.01 level, df 2 | | Insignificant | | | Insignificant | |

The above Table 8.2 reveals that whether the political value is low or high, eunuchs are moderately politically conscious and this consciousness has not been translated into political participation. On anatomising further, it has been found that the insignificant relationships among the above variables were not due to any single reason but due to diffused reasons like low education, callous attitude of society, fear of depletion of livelihood, existence of excessive stress, insecurity, etc. Though the data is not highlighting anything, yet it definitely reflects the fact that high political value causes moderate consciousness and better participation in eunuchs.

**Table 8.3:** Relationship amongst age, political consciousness and political participation of the eunuchs, N–53

| *Age (in years)* | *Political consciousness* | | | *Political participation* | | |
|---|---|---|---|---|---|---|
| | *Low (0–5)* | *Moderate (5–10)* | *High (10–15)* | *Low (0–5)* | *Moderate (5–10)* | *High (10–15)* |
| 18–35 | 2 | 31 | — | 10 | 13 | 10 |
| 36–50 | — | 6 | — | 1 | 1 | 4 |
| 51–65 | — | 7 | 1 | 4 | 2 | 2 |
| Above 65 | — | 6 | — | 6 | — | — |
| $\chi^2$ | | 6.83 | | | 14.94 | |
| Significance at 0.01 level, df 6 | | Insignificant | | | Insignificant | |

The comparison of an independent variable (age) with two dependent variables could not establish any relationship statistically in the present study. Table 8.3 shows that the political consciousness as well as participation was more among young eunuchs i.e., eunuchs in the age-group of 18–35 years. Older eunuchs (above 65 years) were found to be reluctant towards any change in the profession.

The behaviour of aged eunuchs can be interpreted according to their lifestyle perspective. With age, the mobility of eunuchs is halted and their income dries to such an extent that their livelihood completely depends on the income of *akhada*, i.e. from collection which comes through the young eunuchs. Hence, it is observed that mostly aged eunuchs are opposing eunuchs' political participation, whereas young eunuchs are more aspirant and ready for experimentation, especially some alternative careers which might provide them more self-esteem in the society.

**Table 8.4:** Relationship amongst educational level, political consciousness and political participation of the eunuchs, N–53

| *Educational level* | *Political consciousness* | | | *Political participation* | | |
|---|---|---|---|---|---|---|
| | *Low (0–5)* | *Moderate (5–10)* | *High (10–15)* | *Low (0–5)* | *Moderate (5–10)* | *High (10–15)* |
| Illiterate | 1 | 37 | — | 18 | 11 | 9 |
| Primary | — | 7 | 1 | 2 | 1 | 5 |
| Middle | 1 | 3 | — | — | 3 | 1 |
| Secondary | — | 3 | — | 1 | 1 | 1 |
| $\chi^2$ | | 11.64 | | | 9.47 | |
| Significance at 0.01 level, df 6 | | Insignificant | | | Insignificant | |

Education has never been an essential qualification as far as politics is concerned. Same is evident in the case of eunuch aspirants. Shabnam Mausi, Kamala Jaan, Meena Bai, etc. are not properly educated, but they have unusual persistence and initiative, know how to get things done, possess self-confidence and good oratory.

Table 8.4 shows that maximum eunuchs under study were either illiterate or had only primary and their educational status does not bolster the political consciousness and political participation. The computed values of $\chi^2$ in either case is less than the table values, hence, the relationships among the variables are insignificant. From the above it can also be inferred that eunuchs (educated or uneducated) show interest in discussing politics. It may be due to their existing image in the society and a desire to step towards social acceptance to gain mainstream respect.

**Table 8.5:** Media exposure and political consciousness, political participation and political value orientation of the eunuchs, N–53

| *Media exposure* | *Political consciousness* | | | *Political participation* | | | *Political value orientation* | |
|---|---|---|---|---|---|---|---|---|
| | *Low (0–5)* | *Moderate (5–10)* | *High (10–15)* | *Low (0–5)* | *Moderate (5–10)* | *High (10–15)* | *Low (0–8)* | *Moderate (8–16)* |
| Yes | 2 | 46 | 1 | 17 | 16 | 16 | 21 | 28 |
| No | — | 4 | — | 4 | — | — | 3 | 1 |
| $\chi^2$ | | 0.15 | | | 6.57 | | | 144.74 |
| df | | 2 | | | 2 | | | 1 |
| Significance at 0.01 level | | Insignificant | | | Insignificant | | | Significant |

Theoretically media braces political parties and its activities. The effects of media produce higher levels of political knowledge, greater support for campaigns, awareness of the electoral process and motivation for political participation.

Media plays an important role in procuring information about the international, national and local political events. Though media do not normally decide the winner or loser of elections, it influences the outcome. Print media is not that effective as far as eunuchs under study are concerned, due to their illiteracy, whereas audio-visual or electronic media has been found to be more effective and popular among them. Generally, media highlights the effects of politics and portrays its powers and prestige. Therefore, in this case it can be said that the media exposure affects political value orientation significantly but it is just not enough to orient or modulate political awareness among eunuchs and consequently their participation in politics. Their awareness was found to be moderate but it drove them to the polling booths. In fact, eunuch community has its own conflicts, conceptions and misconceptions, hence, the normal media exposure has not proved to be sufficient to motivate the community for active political participation.

Though the above tables anatomised the political behaviour of eunuchs, just bogging into the quantaphenia is not enough to understand their behaviour as eunuchs are individuals with a difference. Stressful events in anybody's life may gash them adrift from their social moorings, resulting in questions like, 'whether life has any meaning'. Eunuchs' lives are full of stresses and such stressful events like experiences of castration, humiliations associated with sexual handicappedness, separation from natal family etc. have potent effect on their lives. One would expect that these difficult experiences would push them away from the self-actualized end of this continuum, as basic needs are the priorities for them. Despite the above fact, a few eunuchs dared to rotate their wheel of fortune especially in the field of politics breaking the monopoly of the mainstream politicians.

Equal political rights were given to eunuchs after independence. Indian legislature took several steps to assign equal status to eunuchs in political field but they are far behind in case of social and economic equality. The preamble to the Constitution promises no discrimination on the basis of sex. Eunuchs derived benefit from these rights and equality with mainstream. The recognition of political equity was undoubtedly a radical departure from the norms prevailing in traditional India. Despite their individualistic radicalism, eunuchs in the suffrage movement were conservative about their community.

The social stigma, illiteracy, sexual handicappedness, incompetency to produce progeny, fear of sexual abuse, lack of family, etc. mingled with their feelings of insecurity, dominance of community norms over heart and brain of eunuchs, abasement and need of succorance generally diminishes the internal locus of control over any event. The experience of emasculation (though almost all eunuchs publicly acclaim that they are congenital eunuch and those who are castrated are not the real one or belong to their community but the fact is occurrence of hermaphrodite is very rare), influences one's socio-political attitudes and actions. Mostly aged eunuchs were found opposing political incarnation of eunuchs. All these factors were found to be dwindling interest in politics and level of information about politics. Though a few eunuchs occupied some important positions in the state of Madhya Pradesh, yet they are considered as a disadvantaged group, translating into lower political efficacy.

In this struggle of recognition, in order to get civil equality along with political equality eunuchs and their action should be fully emancipated along with others' actions and not just as 'eunuch's work' in private and public domain. Then their recognition in society will increase their political consciousness, participation and also their value orientation.

Analysts like Reddy, G. (2003) was very harsh while arguing 'to gain political status *hijras* (eunuchs) are entering the public imagination, explicitly highlighting their social marginality on the basis of their sexuality, religion and kinship'. She argued that *hijras* (eunuchs) apparent increase in political visibility and social status could be illusory and could ultimately serve to remarginalise them within the new social order. Similar chaos was created when women were suffragetting for their rights. As women managed to acquire recognition and self-esteem in the society, now it is eunuchs turn to acquire their appropriate position in the society. Political participation of eunuchs should not be confused with the distrust of public over political parties or any illusion, rather it is the bugle of their emancipation.

During the course of the present study I have observed that the current policies do not address poor health and welfare of this community—they compel the powerless to remain politically voiceless. The biosocial barriers against eunuchs restrict their social, political as well as psychological security in the society. Besides lots of phobias and aversions, eunuchs in India fantasize politics to make their life meaningful and to bring back their dignity which they think is lost when they joined the community. Therefore, the political behaviour of eunuchs should be perceived as a struggle for recognition and self-respect. It is very difficult to arrive at a uniform conclusion or a general statement especially from the present sample, as some comments necessarily are of a speculative nature that is based upon the findings of the present study. Thus, these findings can only be looked at as suggestive and hence, further work ought to be done to follow up this study.

# NINE
# Eunuch Politicians
## A Few Inspirational Profiles

### KAMALA JAAN: FROM *JAAN* TO *MAUSI*

Kamala Jaan struck the headlines after Shabnam Mausi. Kamala Jaan was the first eunuch in democratic India to be elected to the post of Mayor of Katni Municipal Corporation (MP) as an independent candidate in December 1999. She succeeded in trouncing her BJP rival Alka Jain by a margin of 1897 votes for the post, which was reserved for "General Female". It was for the first time that such a post has been held by a eunuch (*hijra*).

The victory of Kamala Jaan astonished people, media and the intelligentsia, and compelled political thinkers to contemplate about the win. Some leaders of political parties commented as 'seemingly curious verdict' of the voters by electing eunuchs. Mr. Prabhat Jha, then BJP state unit media chief said—"the victory of eunuchs showed that the voters were fed up with both politics and politicians".

Katni, a thriving lime stone mining centre was facing severe scarcity of drinking water. Kamala Jaan started running the city with iron hands. She dug wells, improved drainage system, renovated the main bus stand and doled out aid among the poor.

She brushed aside the usually lethargic advisory council members who were supposed to assist her: such behaviour had not been expected from the eunuchs. She refused to take mayoral bungalow. She made use of auto rickshaw fitted with red light on the roof and a driver. People who pursued her voting rolls began to perceive her differently. They started saying that she is unpredictable. She can be abusive because she used to say "if people do not do what you tell them they need to be scolded". But at the same time she was becoming immensely popular among poor and middle class. Unsatisfied opposition sued case against Kamala Jaan, demanding to review her candidature. According to them, the Returning Officer had accepted Kamala Jaan's nomination form without due inquiry and had wrongly declared as returned.

Knowing about my studies on eunuchs, then Additional District Judge Mr. Virender Singh discussed the case regarding the gender of eunuchs with me. I thought I had convinced him that in India almost all eunuchs perceived themselves as female whatever may be their biological status. But judiciary considered their biological or genetically status as 'sex'. As a judge at Katni Court, Mr. Virender Singh ruled that though Kamala Jaan dresses as a woman and believes that she is a female, she is in fact a man and should be disqualified from the Mayoral post, which is reserved under a quota system for general female candidate. However, illiterate Kamala Jaan argued that she is a 'born eunuch' so she should not be considered as a man. But in the decision of 40 pages, the judge agreed with the petitioner that Kamala Jaan is a male. The Madhya Pradesh High Court at Jabalpur ruled that eunuchs are (technically) male, barring them from seeking elected offices reserved for women. Without performing any genetic test, Justice S.P. Khare of the High Court at Jabalpur on Monday, 4 Feb, 2003, upheld a lower court ruling barring Kamala Jaan from becoming Mayor of the Katni because the post was set aside for women. Kamala Jaan was opposed by the spearheaded politicians.

I went to Katni to meet Kamala Jaan. She was simple and very down to earth. Her house was reflecting the same. Though we know each other by name through court cases, we were meeting for the first time. Soon she released her emotions. According to her, she was born in village Mau Tehsil Karvi, District Banda (Uttar Pradesh) in a muslim family. Her father was a farmer. She was born eunuch but brought up like a boy named Kamaluddin. At the age of 12 years she was brought to the community in Katni (MP). Kamala Jaan had been listed as 'male' in some older documents as the electoral rolls of Katni published in 1995. Kamala Jaan had sought entry as a male. In the Election Commission identity card Kamala Jaan is named as Kamal Nihora aged 45 and male but as 'female' in newer ones. Illiterate Kamala Jaan could hardly smell of its repercussions. Here naivety was endeared by the people and soon from '*Jaan*' she became '*mausi*'.

In 1999, on the insistence of local people, especially by Ayaz Khan, a lawyer Kamala Jaan decided to contest Mayoral election. She knew every road of Katni. Her candidature was initially a joke and topic of discussion but later became a serious issue. Gopal Singhania, a journalist persuaded her to contest the election as an independent candidate. A businessman Rajesh Jaiswal funded the campaign, Naresh Khosla, a tailor became campaign manager. Earthen Pot (*Ghara*) became election symbol. Pedal Rickshaw–Auto rickshaw Association, Railway Employees Association and Subhash Gupta's Jan Sahyog Manch, a NGO supported and promoted Kamala Jaan. Drawing crowd was not a problem for Kamala Jaan because of two reasons, first being a eunuch candidate, it was something new for the people of Katni and secondly, frustrated and disgusted with the established political parties, the voters wanted to listen something new. Kamala Jaan won by 1897 votes. Thousands of people attended her victory rally. Kamala, becoming the Mayor of Katni seemed a prank for some people exploratory to others. But for her it was a token to enter into the oasis of respectability.

Dedication of Kamala Mausi threatened the politicians and made them insecure. To let her down questions were raised about her sexuality. Ironically Kamala Jaan failed to prove herself, resulting her relinquishing the chair after four and a half years. Though the landmark judgement against Kamala Jaan discouraged the community, *Mausi* did not give up. In the year 2003 she again contested the election under the banner of Samajwadi Party, this time from Murwara for the post of MLA, which she lost. Kamala Jaan said that as long as the public is with her, she will work for them. According to her, every time she is learning a new lesson, today people know her as a politician.

## SHABNAM MAUSI: AN INSPIRATION FOR THE ENTIRE COMMUNITY

It was in the year 2005, before I had met with the actual Shabnam Mausi. I met with the on screen Shabnam Mausi i.e., Ashutosh Rana the Hindi movie actor. It just happened that one evening I went to my journalist cum friend's chamber where I found Ashutosh Rana already sitting there, he had come to promote his film *'Shabnam Mausi'* directed by Yogesh Bhardwaj. He played the lead role of Shabnam Mausi. Before I met with actual Shabnam Mausi I knew her through Ashutosh Rana, his film, news and internet. Shabnam Mausi promulgated everywhere.

When I actually met with Mausi, it amazed me as I found her very simple in a *'lungi'* and a sandow vest against my envision. Initially she thought I was a *'film wala'* and started abusing the director and producer of the film 'Shabnam Mausi' for not paying the promised amount. When I introduced myself the outspoken Mausi composed herself and met me very cordially. I found her more talented, shrewd, canny, outspoken and experienced politician than others. She shared her entire peregrination of life from Mumbai society to the centre of M.P. politics.

Shabnam Mausi was born in a Brahmin family in Mumbai. Her father Gokul Prasad Sharma was a Police officer who after retirement is living in Kanpur (UP) and her mother was a post graduate in Sanskrit. She was brought up as a boy named

Chandra Prakash Sharma. She studied upto class 2 in a school of Mumbai, but soon her sexual status denuded from her gestures and postures. She was born eunuch. At the age of 9, she joined eunuch community. Ram Chandra of Mumbai was her first *guru*. She was reared by a poor scheduled tribe (KOL). Lateron, after wandering in many cities she settled down in Anuppur, District Shahdol of Madhya Pradesh.

Shabnam can speak 11 languages including English, Hindi, Marathi, Gujarati, Punjabi, Kannada, Telugu and Tamil. She earned her bread and butter through the traditional profession of the community i.e. singing and dancing on auspicious occasions. She also danced in few Bollywood films like Amar Akbar Anthony, Don and Janata Hawaldar.

In Anuppur Shabnam began to establish herself as *Guru*. Within few years she became leader in the local community. She used her money to sponsor rituals of adopted relations like marriages, etc. of adopted daughters, in neighbourhood etc. She tried to enhance her reputation in the society by constructing a Saibaba Temple. To transform societal scorn into respect she attempted politics too.

The people of Anuppur wanted her to contest election from Anuppur constituency, but the seat was declared reserved for scheduled tribes. So she selected Sohagpur, district Shahdol, as it was for general category. Voters of Sohagpur constituency created history of sorts by electing Shabnam Mausi, a eunuch as their MLA in the by polls held on February 18, 2000. Contesting as an independent candidate, she defeated her closet rival, Mr. Lallu Singh of the BJP by 17,863 votes. Shabnam Mausi got 39,937 (44.07%) and Lallu Singh of BJP got 22,074 (24.36%) and Brijesh Singh of Congress got 17,282 (19.07%) votes. Shabnam Mausi became the first eunuch MLA of India.

On the very first day as MLA, she tabled a call attention motion in the assembly. She said "my constituents are poor, illiterate tribals of Shahdol. There is no pension for old, hopeless women, no jobs for the youngsters who are forced into the world of crime. I want to know what the government is doing for them. She took her assignment as God's wish. She decided to raise voice against corrupt politicians in her own style, sometimes in assembly, sometimes media and sometimes with typical '*Hijra Clap*'." She accused former PWD Minister Bisahu Lal Singh for Shahdol's battered roads. Shabnam Mausi and Bisahu Lal Singh became antagonist thereafter. On many fronts, whether it was on public platform or in corridors of Vidhan Sabha' they confronted each other.

In the two and half year tenure Shabnam Mausi realized that as an independent MLA, she did not get much cooperation from the Government of ruling party though she is thankful to Mr. Pankaj Agrawal, Collector, Shahdol for his support. In the next election i.e. in 2003 she couldn't prove herself, she got only 1401 votes.

In 2008 she joined Lalu Prasad Yadav's political party Rashtriya Janata Dal (RJD). Lalu declared her name for the election from Kotama seat, District Anuppur (M.P.).

Though Shabnam Mausi contested elections several times but she couldn't achieve the position she wanted. In the year 2012, she changed the state i.e. UP this time she contested from Kanpur Cantt under Rashtriya Vikang Party (RVP) and could manage to get only 118 votes and lost the security deposit.

In spite of her failure in election, she did not give up the struggle of self-identity. Perhaps soon she will realize that winning election is different from politics. Winning election is simply the management of votes, now a days it has nothing to do with social service. Sooner or later Shabnam and other eunuchs will also understand this fact and will be crowned with success.

## SURAIYA NAYAK: A EUNUCH WITH VISION

Suraiya is one of the colourful contestants of the state capital Bhopal. In a colourful Salwar Kameej, though awkwardly draped around her masculine figure. At a first glance she appeared to be a woman. She is comparatively a richer eunuch, so is her '*akhada*'. She is the owner of a big mansion in Mangalwara area of Bhopal. She loves to show off and has a liking for glamour. When I tried to take her picture she stopped me saying that she was not ready. She provided me many of her photographs with full make up. I sensed she is different from the rest of the eunuch politicians. She was shrewd, sharp and manipulative while accompanying Shabnam Mausi on the corridor of Vidhan Sabha she dreamt of becoming a politician. She knows her drawbacks, every time she smartly escaped talking about her past life, but she wanted to establish herself as a politician.

First, she tried to unite all eunuch aspirants who saw their future in politics. She talked to leading political parties for tickets but didn't get success. So she along with other eunuch politicians, decided to launch their own political party named Jiti Jitai Party (JJP) i.e. already won party. Her motive was to unite all the ambitious eunuch politicians and provide them a platform. For Suraiya, the electoral battle should not be confined to Bhopal only. She wanted to build a national party for eunuchs and enter Parliament. In October 2003, JJP declared that eunuchs will contest from 55 seats in next state's election. Suraiya also announced that she will contest from Bhopal North constituency, which was a general seat. Unfortunately, by that time the party was not registered. Her symbol was a 'Book' She argued that the lives of eunuchs are open book. With the blessings of her Guru Prem Nayak she initiated her campaign. Her favourite axiom during the election was, '*Suraiya Khari Chunav Main Sab Ki Mange Khair, Naa Kahu Sang Dosti Naa Kahoo Sang Bair*' (I beseech blessings for all, I have no favourites: neither have I friends nor have I foes). She promised that after becoming MLA, she would fight against corruption. According to her, the sitting MLA and a Minister of Gas relief Mr. Arif Akeel had done nothing for North Bhopal. She promised to open schools, hospitals and increase avenues of employment.

While filing the nomination papers as an independent candidate, she was accompanied by huge supporters. But in that crowd one of her eunuchs friend's bag was snatched. After this incident she was provided police protection. Like an accomplished politicians she campaigned from door to door. She was weighed with fruits in Nav Bahar Sabji Mandi

(Vegetable Market) by traders and hawker. In her speech she used to pass sarcastic comments as 'in politics there are many fake eunuchs who are making money through corruption'.

In spite of her crowd puling capacity, she failed to convert it into sufficient votes. In the state election of 2003 she could manage only 974 votes. As politicians, eunuchs failed but for the novice who was deprived of basic rights and necessities for centuries, it was a new beginning and a positive omen.

### BANO JAAN: TRYING TO BLOOM LOTUS IN A DESERT

Bano was born as a boy in a lower middle class family. Besides going to school, Bano used to enjoy the company of 'bad boys'. One day without telling anybody Bano left the home along with a friend. Soon she realized it was a blunder on her part. At the age of 18 she was castrated and became permanent member of the community at Rewa. Now Bano is a *guru* of her *Akhada* and has four disciples. When I reached Rewa, Bano Jaan was already a well-known personality. It didn't take much time or effort to reach her place. She was simple but focused. Although Bano Jaan is respected in her community, she still has guilt feelings about the way she had disgraced her parents and family. The wind of politics in the eunuch community sprouted new hope in the deserted life of Bano Jaan. Inspired by former Prime Minister Shri Atal Bihari Vajpayee, Bano and her four disciples formally joined BJP i.e. Bhartiya Janata Party. Though Bano sensed that they (eunuchs) are not treated in the same way as the other members of the party, yet she felt that it is better to have a party's name or support rather than remaining an independent. In 2003 states' elections, Bano Jaan contested from Rewa as BJP candidate. She lost the seat, she got 1797 votes. She said votes are new route for social recognition. She also said that she will try again as her success in politics will bring back the honour and pride of her family. She said "I want to return the money I gathered from public in so many years by singing and dancing, through social services. I didn't ask for any financial support for election from any one, only asked for their blessings. As it was my first time in politics, I might have committed mistakes. But I got the path to retrieve my self-esteem, I will keep trying in politics". She was worried for Rewa, accordingly though Rewa was under kingship for a long time. It has not been developed as other cities of Madhya Pradesh like Indore, Bhopal, Jabalpur and Gwalior. So she wants to dedicate herself for the development of Rewa and would like to continue to serve the people.

## KAMALA BUA: VICTIM OF PREJUDICE

When I reached Sagar to visit Kamala Bua, I was not sure, it would be convenient for a public personal so early in the morning, but she was on her duty. I was escorted to the lake of Sagar, where I found a middle aged, bulky, Kamala Bua in white Salwar Kameez, surrounded by supporters, busy in cleansing the lake. Because of the scarcity of water, she intended to clear that before summer, so as to make it suitable for proper usage as drinking and cooking. From the very first encounter one can make out that Kamala Bua is a popular leader. The journey of Kamala Bua from eunuch to a popular leader is very interesting. During this journey, love for Sagar and its people acted as catalyst.

"Friends, I am a eunuch and am deprived of nature's gift. As India is a country of faiths and beliefs, I feel that perhaps I have committed some blunder in my past life and that could be one reason, why I have been cursed to become a eunuch. But I am not pessimistic. I am grateful to the almighty. As a eunuch I got opportunity to adore people, bless them for their betterment and prosperity. It is said that god accepts worship of eunuchs before anyone else as they pray for the betterment of other people. I have no other business and family, entire Sagar is my family. I pray for the people of Sagar, its development and prosperity."

Above is the portion of Kamala Bua's appeal (Translated to English during her election campaign) it touched the soul of the people of Sagar so much that they showed their faith and love by electing her as Mayor, though she had contested as an independent candidate.

Kamala Bua became the second eunuch Mayor in the history of Madhya Pradesh. Ten years ago her namesake Kamala Jaan was elected as Mayor of Katni. Kamala Bua was a born eunuch. She became part of community when she was only two months old. She was born in Sagar in 1950 in a scheduled caste family (*Kori*). She was the eldest among four siblings. Her parents were illiterates and *Beedi* workers by profession. Being a local she had great affinity with Sagar.

She was inspired by the honesty of the late Prime Minister Smt. Indra Gandhi and Shri Atal Behari Bajpai. But the corruption and anarchy in Sagar instigated Kamala Bua to join a political party. Though Kamala Bua was illiterate and did not get opportunity for proper education (as she was brought to the community when she was only two months old) she is politically an aware person. Conversations with Kamala Bua on politics were quite interesting as she contemplated politics very keenly and closely. She was very frank and bold and shared her views on various political issues.

She said eunuchs were used as pawns in politics like Shabnam Mausi was used by Bisahulal Sahu and Kamala Jaan by some selfish people. According to her—eunuchs should join politics only for social service. Her self-confidence and determination for the welfare of Sagar drove her to active politics. She learned lessons from the political graph of Shabnam Mausi and Kamala Jaan. Due to humble and polite nature Kamala became popular and managed to receive the confidence of the public. She drew huge crowds for her election campaign where voters could be seen touching her feet.

In 2009 Kamala Bua contested election for the post of Mayor in Sagar Municipal Corporation in Madhya Pradesh as an independent candidate. The post of Sagar Mayor was reserved for Scheduled Caste female. For the past 25 years Kamala Bua had voted as a 'female', she was registered on the voters list as female. Moreover, she is '*kori*' by caste so she became eligible for the candidature. Kamala won the election with a huge margin, she bagged more than 60 per cent of the votes polled. She defeated her nearest BJP rival Suman Ahirwar with a record margin of over 47000 votes. The BJP was holding the post for the past 10 years.

From past experiences Kamala Bua had anticipated unknown controversy conspiracy, so applied for 'caveat' in the High Court at Jabalpur. Very soon a petition was filed by the former Municipal Commissioner of Burhanpur, Shri Mahendra Rai challenging her caste and sex. During trial, it came to light that while filing nomination form, Kamala Bua had clearly mentioned 'without caste eunuch' in the column of caste. But the returning officer, then Additional Collector Rajesh Kaul had asked Kamala to correct it and write '*Kori*' for her caste. The court, in its judgement, observed, that this was the fault of the returning officer, who instead of rejecting the nomination paper, had asked Kamala Bua to mention her caste. The returning officer should have used the discretionary powers. Advocate Singh informed that eunuchs can contest election on the seats which are unreserved, but on seats reserved on caste basis, they cannot fight as they do not have any caste. (After this case Election Commission of India amended its rules, a third option of 'others' has been added on the voters list registered form. The election of Kamala Bua was declared null).

Kamala Bua felt victimized and felt bad for those who voted for her. She said that she is strong enough and is having supporters, she will definitely contest next election, whether it is for the state assembly or the Parliament. She added everybody knows how much she loves Sagar. She will continue to work for the people in future also.

## Appendix

### *Before the Court of First Additional District Judge, Katni Presided by Shri Virender Singh*

(Translated from Hindi)

**Election Petition No. 12/2000.**

1. Sadiq Ali S/o Syed Mustaq Ali
   Age — 34 years,
   R/o — Ram Niwas Singh ward, Katni
2. Radha Sahu W/o Shri Suresh Sahu
   Age—36 years,
   R/o—Chhakodilal Pathak ward, Katni

**Election Petition No. 13/2000.**

1. Rajendra Agarwal S/o Surya Narayan Agrawal
   Age — 37 years,
   R/o — Nehru ward, Katni
2. Smt. Rajeshwari Wankhede W/o Shyamrao Wankhede
   R/o—Ramniwas Singh ward, Katni

**Election Petition No. 18/2000.**

1. Smt. Kiran Gupta W/o Shri Rajaram Gupta
   Age—36 years,
   R/o—E.W.S. Quarter,
   Housing Board Colony, Katni
2. Kamendra Singh
   S/o Late Shri Bahadur Singh Thakur,
   Age—36 years,
   R/o —Malviyaganj, Katni

**Election Petition No. 21/2000.**

1. Naresh Bhatia S/o Shri Shankarlal Bhatia
   Age—37 years,
   R/o—28 M.I.G. Housing Board Colony, Katni
2. Rajaram Gupta S/o Shyamlal Gupta
   Age—34 years,
   R/o—E.W.S. Quarter, Housing Board Colony, Katni

*Petitioners.*

*Versus*

1. Kamala @ Kamala Jaan Hijra Father/Guru Nihora
   Mayor, Katni Municipal Corporation,
   R/o—Behind Mosque, Subhash ward, Katni
2. Smt. Aradhana Rakesh Jain W/o Rakesh Jain
   R/o—Nai Basti, Sawarkar ward, Katni
3. Smt. Alka Jain W/o Dr. Shikhar Jain
   R/o—27 M.I.G., Housing Board Colony, Katni
4. Ms. Taslim Bano Khan D/o Unknown
   R/o—Near Syed Baba's Shrine,
   Mission Chawk, Ishwaripura Ward, Katni
5. Smt. Saroj Bachchan Nayak
   W/o Shri Bachchan Nayak
   R/o—10, Sawarkar Ward,
   Nai Basti, Katni
6. Smt. Sushma Ram Mohan Shivhare, Advocate
   W/o Shri Ram Mohan Shivhare,
   R/o—Near Laxminarayan Temple,
   Azad Chawk, Katni

*Respondents.*

**Election Petition No. 14/2000.**

Ku. Namita Chauhan D/o Shri Amrit Singh Chauhan
Age—About 21 years,
R/o—Raghunath Ganj ward, Sukkhan Akhada, Katni

*Petitioners.*

*Versus*

1. Kamala Jaan @Hijra Father's name unknown
   Age—About 48 years,
   R/o—Alfertganj ward, Near Mosque, Katni
2. Smt. Alka Jain W/o Dr. Shikhar Jain
   Age—About 42 years,
   R/o—Nehru ward,
   27, M.I.G. Housing Board Colony, Katni
3. Smt. Aradhana Jain W/o Rakesh Jain
   Age—29 years,
   R/o—Sawarkar ward, Nai Basti, Katni
4. Ms. Taslim Bano Khan D/o Mohd. Haneef
   Age—About 28 years,
   R/o—Ishwaripura ward,
   Near Syed Baba's Shrine, Katni
5. Smt. Saroj Nayak W/o Shri Bachchan Nayak
   Age—About 45 years,
   R/o—10, Sawarkar ward, Nai Basti, Katni
6. Smt. Sushma Shivhare
   W/o Shri Ram Mohan Shivhare,
   Age—About 37 years,
   R/o—Near Laxminarayan Temple,
   Purani Basti, Katni
7. Returning Officer, the Collector,
   Municipal Corporation, Katni
   State of M.P.
   Through the Collector, Katni

(*Note*: Respondent Nos. 7 & 8 were deleted *vide* order dated 13/11/2000)

## JUDGMENT

(Pronounced on 29.8.2002)

1. All the above five election petitions have been presented disputing the same election, on the basis of identical facts, against the same respondents and for almost the identical relief, hence for the sake of convenience; all are being decided by a common judgment.
2. All the above election petitions have been filed assailing the election for the post of Mayor of the Municipal Corporation Katni held in the year 1999 under Section 441 M.P. Municipal Corporation Act. 1956 read with Municipal Corporation (Election Petition) Rules 1963, in which respondent no. 1 was declared returned, mainly on the ground that the office of Mayor was reserved for woman and respondent no. 1 is not a woman.
3. These facts are not in dispute between the parties that in the year 1999 Mayor of Katni Municipal Corporation was to be elected and this office was reserved for woman of general category and in this regard a notification was issued. Nomination for election was filed on 02.12.1999 it was accepted on 03.12.1999 and 22.12.1999 was fixed for voting. Respondent no. 1 to 6 had submitted nomination papers for the same. After voting on 22.12.1999, counting took place on 27.12.1999 and respondent no. 1 secured 23215 votes, no. 3 secured 21418, no. 2 secured 12943, no. 5 secured 7832, no. 4 got 4591 and respondent no. 6 secured 239 votes and respondent no.1 was declared returned as the highest votes catcher.
4. The facts of the petition in short are that the petitioners are voters of Katni Municipal Corporation area. Election for the office of Mayor of Katni Municipal Corporation was to be held in the year 1999 and for this, nominations were filed on 02.12.1999, nominations were scrutinized on 03.12.1999 and 22.12.1999 was fixed

for voting. Under the Reservation Rules framed by the Government of M.P., the office of Mayor of Katni Municipal Corporation was reserved for "General Female" candidate hence only female candidates were eligible to contest election to this office. The respondent no. 1 had submitted nomination paper for election by mentioning self as a woman, whereas the concerned person was "*hijra*" and not a "female". This nomination paper was wrongly accepted by the election officer without any scrutiny and vide Gazette notification dated 31.12.1999 issued by the Government of M.P. was wrongly declared elected hence a prayer has been made to declare the election as void.

5. It has also been stated by the petitioners that respondent no. 1 was not a born woman. The person has declared self in the nomination paper as "*hijra*" which is an own admission. According to medical science "*hijra*" does not mean "female". As per Medical Jurisprudence and Toxicology of Dr. S.S. Daniel and Shri D.K. Tiwari, such a person can never be a woman. In the census of the Government of India also, eunuch has been categorized as male. The name of the respondent no. 1 is mentioned in part 2 of the voter list of ward no. 25 at Sr. no. 643 as Kamala, father/husband Nihora, "male" aged 48 yrs. The entry at Sr. no. 644 as Kamala father/husband unknown "female" is not of respondent no. 1. As per the custom prevailing in eunuch community, a disciple gets the seat and property of the *guru*. On the basis of this custom, respondent no. 1 has succeeded to the property of the *guru*. Prior to 1993 Nihora was recognized as *guru* of *Katni Hijra Sangh*. After the *guru*'s death respondent no. 1 took over as *guru* that is why respondent no. 1 has been mentioned as Kamala parenthood Nihora. Among the Muslim, it is prohibited for women to perform *namaz* in mosque but respondent no. 1 performs *namaz* at mosque, from this, it is apparent that the respondent is a male. On all these grounds it

has been prayed to quash the election of respondent no. 1 as the person is a male. Some petitioners have prayed for declaring the election of respondent no. 1 as void and to declare respondent no. 3 as returned.

6. Petitioner Namita Chauhan has further stated that respondent no. 1 is male eunuch. Kamala is concealing the true identity as male eunuch and is bearing female looks and earning livelihood by dancing and singing. The above person has cheated 23215 voters of Katni region by declaring self as woman. If it was not declared so falsely, none would have voted for Kamala. Because of his false declaration, voters have been deprived from using their rights of franchise correctly, hence, the election of Mayor has been substantially affected. This petitioner has prayed for cancellation of the election.

7. Respondent no. 1 has stated in a written statement submitted that she is a "woman" and "eunuch" is her nick name. She had filed her nomination as woman of General category, which was accepted as legal. It was further stated that respondent no. 1 was woman since birth. Eunuch society has found her orphan and was brought up by them and kept her in their occupation. Because of love and affection received from them she added the nickname "eunuch" to her name. Ever since the filing of nomination paper by her till the declaration of result, none had raised any objection regarding her womanhood. The voter list was prepared in the year 1994 by the Municipal Corporation Katni long ago before this disputed election. The respondent no. 1 had mentioned her name in the same, which is mentioned at voter no. 125. House no. 124 as woman in the part 2 of the amended list of ward no. 25 Netaji Subhash Chandra Ward. In the voter list prepared again in the year 1999, her name was mentioned as woman. The respondent no.1 has stated that the petitioners have falsely mentioned in the petition that entry at Sr. no.643 in the voter list as Kamala Nihora, is of respondent no. 1. In the amended list of 1994, no person of this name

was added, she is not aware as to how this name was added or got included in the voter list of 1994. Respondent no. 1 is not Kamala parenthood Nihora, neither she knew him nor does she has any relation with him, any person of this name is neither in existence at present or was in the past. It does not make any difference that eunuchs have been classed in male category during census because respondent no. 1 is female. The data recorded during the census have no legal value. The persons of eunuch community normally adopt Muslim religion hence respondent no. 1 also adopted Muslim religion while living with them, and being a woman, she performs *namaz* at home and has never visited mosque to perform *namaz*.

8. Respondent no. 1 is a female since birth. According to the respondent medical tests violate the limits of her modesty, morality and *purdah* status. These things along with being divine, are also recognized as social and legal rights, hence until a person agrees, she should not be compelled for medical tests. Opinion of other medical jurists are not similar to the opinion given in Medical Jurisprudence of Dr. Daniel and Shri Tiwari. On the basis of the voice and physique of a person, he can't be presumed to be of masculine gender. Similarly, by using the nickname eunuch, presumption of eunuch cannot be drawn. She is a woman of general category hence, her election is valid.
9. Respondent no. 1 has also stated that as per the provisions of sub-Section 2(3) of Section 441 of Madhya Pradesh Municipal Corporation Act. 1956, the jurisdiction to hear the election petitions against the respondent no.1 lies with the Principal Civil Court, this court has no jurisdiction to hear the petitions. The petitions are not properly verified and drawn and therefore, are not maintainable. No objection has been filed against the nomination or election of respondent no. 1 under the provisions and rules of Municipal Corporation Act. 1956 till the declaration of election

result, hence the present petitions are not maintainable and prayer has been made to dismiss the petitions on these grounds.

10. Respondent no. 2 and 6 have admitted all the facts of the petition including the relief. By way of additional statement, they have just stated that in the English Dictionary, the meaning of the word "eunuch" is 'a castrated male person'. But Sr. no. 186 of the voter list of 1994 of assembly election and in the Election ID Card no. 402105, the name of respondent no.1 stands recorded as a male person. They have prayed to cancel the suit election and to order fresh polls amongst the remaining respondents.

11. Respondent no. 3 has also admitted the facts of the petition and the relief clause. However, as an additional statement, she has stated that on page no. 25 of the Census Booklet 1991 issued by the Census Commissioner, Government of India, it has been specifically instructed to show eunuchs as male persons. At Sr. no. 186 of the voter list pertaining to Subhash Ward, Katni of Assembly Constituency no. 202 as contained in the Madhya Pradesh Voters bye-laws, 1995, Kamal Nihol stands recorded as a male. In the amended voter list appended thereto, Kamal Nihol has been amended as Kamala Nihora but gender has not been amended as to a female one. Even in the voter list, 1998 of Assembly Constituency, Katni, at Sr.no. 185, Subhash ward, Katni, the gender of Kamala Nihora is recorded as "male". The Election Commission of India issued the Voter's Identity Card in 1995. Identity Card no. 402105 was issued in the name of respondent no.1 and therein also his name has been recorded as a male person. The said Identity Card also carries the photograph of respondent no. 1. In the voters list also, it has been mentioned that Identity Card was issued. The respondent no.1 has never attempted to amend the said entry in the identity card.

12. Respondent no.1 has been living in Subhash Ward

Katni for about last 20 years and during all these years he has cast his vote as "Kamala Nihora" male in all Parliamentary, Assembly and Municipal Elections. He has never attempted to amend the entry of his gender during the said period.

13. According to the respondent no. 3, their *panch* members of eunuchs community have unanimously decided that after the demise of *guru* of their eunuchs community, respondent no.1 be appointed as true heir of the seat of *guru* Nihora and information to this effect was published by their community in the widely circulated eveninger of Katni "*Dainik Madhya Pradesh*" in the issue dated 12.12.1993 and the respondent no.1 had not rebutted that.
14. That the name of respondent no.1 stands recorded as male at Sr. no. 643 of the voter list of Subhash ward, Katni issued by the Municipal Corporation. Despite this information, he has concealed his identity and submitted his nomination form at Sr. no. 644 in the name of Kamala as the child of some unknown female. Thus, the respondent no.1 has voluntarily suppressed facts before the Returning Officer and submitted false declaration and the nomination form was accepted wrongfully without due inquiry.
15. The respondent has also stated that, had the nomination form of the respondent no. 1 was rejected, she would have been definitely declared as returned. Because, after respondent no. 1, she (respondent no. 3) secured the maximum votes (21,418), therefore, the respondent no. 3 has prayed to declare the election of respondent no.1 as void and declare her as elected.
16. *Ex parte* proceedings have been taken against respondent no. 4. Her application to set aside the same has been rejected and, therefore, she submitted a written statement at a subsequent stage but that was not taken on record. However, she has described the contents stated in her petition as true and prayed to declare the election as void. She has also opposed the

relief claimed by respondent no. 3 to declare self as returned and also raised objections to the effect that the Returning Officer, Katni is a necessary party and due to nonjoinder of parties, the election petition is not maintainable.

17. Respondent no. 5 has been proceeded *ex parte* and no written statement/return has been submitted on her behalf.
18. On the basis of pleadings of either parties, the following issues have been framed, the findings of which are mentioned against them in brief and their discussion with reasoning is as follows:

| *Sr. No.* | *Issue* | *Findings* |
|---|---|---|
| 1 | Whether respondent no.1 is not a female? | No |
| 2 | Whether respondent no.1 was eligible to contest the election? | No |
| 3 | Whether the Returning Officer erred in accepting the nomination form of the respondent no.1 for the suit election? | Yes |
| 4 | Whether the election of respondent no.1 in the said election is void? | Yes |
| 5 | Whether respondent no.3 deserves to be declared returned? | No |
| 6 | Whether this petition is not maintainable due to non-raising of objections during the entire process of election? | It is maintainable |
| 7 | Whether this court enjoys jurisdiction to hear this petition? | Yes |
| 8 | Relief and costs | Petitions admitted, election declared void and no candidate declared returned |

## GROUNDS OF FINDINGS

### *Issue nos. 6 & 7*

19. Both these issues have been determined together as preliminary issues on 06.12.2000 and accordingly, rejecting both the objections of respondent no.1, this petition has already been held to be maintainable

before this court. Order of this court has not been challenged and, therefore, both these issues are decided in negation against the respondent no.1.

20 Respondent has cited in this regard several judicial illustrations viz. **JLJ 1973 Note 16 MP (DB) Mangu Vs. Returning Officer, AIR 1988 SC 1796 Birad Mal Singhvi Vs. Anand Purohit, AIR 1988 SC 637 Shiv Charan Singh Vs. Chandra Bhan Singh, AIR 1990 NOC 109 (Guwahati) Dr. Purna Narayan Singh Vs. Golak Nath and AIR 1985 SC 847 Brij Mohan Vs. Satpal.** Out of these, the first two have no application in the present case due to difference in facts and in the remaining ones, it has been held either to admit election petitions despite non-raising of an objection against the acceptance of nomination form directly or indirectly or in other cases, election petitions have been admitted.

21. As per Section 441-B (1) (d) (i) of Municipal Corporation Act, a petition shall lie against improper acceptance of a nomination form.

22. In **1996 MPLJ 967 State Election Commission Vs. Ras Bihari Raghuwanshi**, Hon'ble Court has held that grounds of improper acceptance of nomination form or rejection thereof may be raised in the election petitions. Otherwise too, in the light of the order dated 06.12.2000, the arguments advanced by the respondents doesn't gain ground.

### *Issue nos.1 to 4*

23. All these issues are being dealt and determined jointly for being interconnected and for the sake of convenience and to avoid repetition of evidence.

24. The focal point of all the instant election petitions is that whether the respondent no. 1 (hereinafter referred to as the "Respondent" only) is a female or not? The entire dispute revolves around this issue. Obviously, the other parties have advanced arguments to free themselves from the onus of proof and to shift them

on the other side. The respondent has relied upon Section 101 and 102 of the Evidence Act, whereas, the petitioner has banked upon Section 106. On the basis of these provisions only, the respondent has argued that the onus of proving the facts stated in the petition lies on the petitioners whereas, the petitioners contend that this fact is particularly known to the respondent and, therefore, respondent has to prove it.

25. Whenever we apply the test of Section 101 of the Evidence Act, it becomes clear that petitioners have sought relief of declaration of a statutory right or obligation and they have sought such a declaration on the basis of fact that the respondent is not a female and, therefore, he has to prove the same. It is even clear while testing this case on the parameters of Section 102 of the Evidence Act that if either parties do not adduce evidence, the petitioners would definitely loose. From this point of view also, the burden of proving lies on them only. So far as Section 106 of the Evidence Act is concerned, findings of Hon'ble Supreme Court of India are worth noting in this regard given in **AIR 1975 SC 667 Ch. Razik Ram Vs. Ch. J.S. Chouhan**, Hon'ble Court has held in that case that though election petitions are different from Sessions Trial, yet the onus of proving every fact against every allegations lies on the petitioner himself. If any such fact forming relevant fact of law is in particularly within the knowledge of the respondent, in that case, this affects the quantum of the onus of proof but does not exonerate petitioner from his primary liability. Petitioner in that case will have to produce prima facie evidence in relation to the fact.

26. This issue has been decided in the proceeding order dated 16.08.2001 that burden of proof primarily lies with the petitioners and that proceeding order has not been challenged in any way by the petitioners.

27. Keeping in view the fact and circumstances of the present case regarding the burden of proving, Hon'ble

Court has clarified the position in an important citation **AIR 1964 SC 880 Kalwa Devadattam and others Vs. Union of India and others** holding that the question of onus of proving becomes very important at the primary stage of the case and it becomes even more important when neither of the parties to the dispute adduce any evidence. Under these circumstances, the party which is required to prove looses. But where the opposite parties have adduced evidence regarding issues, the questions of burden or proving becomes *infructuous* and in such cases, the truthfulness or otherwise of the case should be decided on the basis of appreciation of evidences produced by the parties. In the light of that citation, the questions of onus of proof at this stage of the case is not important and relevant. Citation of **Premlata Vs. Arhant Kumar AIR 1972 SC 626** is also worth mentioning.

28. The respondent has raised the other two objections regarding verification of the petition and cause of action. She has stated that petitions have not been lawfully verified and cause of action is not mentioned therein. In this regard, following citations have been produced viz. **2002 (1) JLJ 245 Hari Singh Narwariya Vs. Rakesh Shukla, 2000 (1) Supreme 290 V. Narayanaswami Vs. C.P. Thirunavukkarasu, AIR 1987 SC 1926 Samar Singh Vs. Kedar Nath, 1986 (2) MPWN 53 = AIR 1986 SC 1534 Bhagwati Prasad Dixit Ghorewala Vs. Rajeev Gandhi.** It has been held in all these citations that in the election petitions presented on the grounds of corrupt practices, it is mandatory to make mention of all those relevant facts which form corrupt practice. The requirement of verification of the pleadings has also been emphasized in the citations. In the last three citations, jurisdiction to quash the petitions has been clarified in default of cause of action at the preliminary stage or under Order 7 Rule 11 of the CPC, even after framing of the issues.

29. In the light of these citations and upon perusal of the

facts of the case in that backdrop, it is clear that in para no. 11 of the petitioner no.14/2000, cause of action is clearly stated. In other petitions, though it is not clearly stated, para no.11 makes definite mention. Though the words "cause of action" are not used yet, the complete mention of the relevant fact figure in the petitions. The respondent herself has stated that in the citation **2000 (1) Supreme 290 (Supra)** it has been held by the Hon'ble Court that the courts must see whether any cause of action or determinable issues arises in the said petitions or not. Hon'ble Court has also held in **Jethmal Vs. Hiralal and others AIR 1972 Rajasthan 220** that on the basis of other facts stated in the plaint regarding cause of action, the courts may decide *suo motu* the date of cause of action. It has been clarified in several other citations by the Hon'ble Court that it is the duty of the courts to inquire about the whole statements of the plaintiff to ascertain cause of action. No presumption can be drawn merely in absence of words "cause of action".

30. Verification of the petition no.14/2000 fully conforms to law. No infirmity has been shown. It is true that in other petitions, the petitioners have not separately disclosed as to which of the fact stated in petition para nos.1 to 17 is true as per their own knowledge and which are stated on the basis of information secured by them. This verification does not strictly adhere to order 6 R 15 Sub Rule 2 of the CPC but on that basis alone, petitions cannot be dismissed.

31. In **Devi Prasad Vs. Chairman of the Court of Election Tribunal, Gorakhpur and another AIR 1956 Allahabad 19**, it has been held that infirmity or omissions in the verification does not amount to illegality but amounts to an irregularity which may be cured by way of amendment. This infirmity does not affect jurisdiction of the election authority. According to **AIR 1934 Calcutta 632**, such verification that, fact stated in the plaint is true as per the knowledge and

belief of the plaintiff irrespective of disclosure of the source of information, fully satisfies the provisions of Order 6 Rule 15 of the CPC. According to **AIR 1959 Calcutta 642,** whenever any pleading falls short of this provision, the infirmity is only an irregularity and may be cured by amendment. As per citation **AIR 1964 J&K 88,** no petition is rendered illegal merely on the ground of petitioner's failure to state in the petition as to which particular para of the petition is verified as per his own knowledge and which is verified as per the information secured from other sources and on that basis only, petition cannot be dismissed. In **Bhikaji Keshao Joshi Vs. Brijlal Nandlal Biyani AIR 1955 SC 610,** it has been held that defect of date of verification cannot be a ground for dismissal of a petition. In **Krishan Chander Vs. Ram Lal (1973) 2 SCC 759,** it is clarified that it is not necessary to state right to obtain information in an election petition.

32. In this way, the cause of action is clearly stated in petition No. 14/2000 and its verification conforms to law. In other petitions, all the relevant facts and elements exist. Therefore, on the basis of these technical objections, petitions cannot be dismissed.
33. The respondent has also raised another objection that only one petitioner Kamendra Singh has examined himself in support of the petition, therefore, the other petitions are liable to be dismissed in default of statements of the petitioners but vide Order dated 13.11.2000, all the petitions have been clubbed. All the petitions have been heard under one petition 12/2000 All the petitions are based on the common facts and even the relevant relief is identical. Under these circumstances, these cannot be dismissed for want of statement of other petitioners. Therefore, this objection of the respondents is overruled.
34. It becomes clear from the appreciation of evidence pertaining to the dispute between the parties that according to petitioners, the respondent Kamala, child

of Nihora, is eunuch, whereas, the respondent stated that the woman-parenthood of Kamala is unknown. Respondent no. 1 has vehemently opposed that self is Kamala, parenthood Nihora but has not refuted that Kamala, parenthood of Nihora was a eunuch.

35. As regards the fact that respondent no. 1 alone is Kamala parenthood of Nihora, Kamendra Singh (PW1) states that after the death of *guru* Nihora in 1993 dispute and rivalry took place amongst the eunuchs and thereafter a convention was called wherein according to *panch nirnaya,* the respondent was elected as successor of Nihora. The news item of this was published along with photograph and decision of the *panch* members in the issue dated 12.9.1993 of the daily "*Dainik Madhya Pradesh*". As per the tradition prevalent amongst eunuchs, in place of father's name, name of the *guru* is stated and, therefore, respondent's father is shown as "Nihora". After nomination as successor, the property of the Nihora including building no. 124 situated in Subhash Ward (ward no. 20) was accrued by him. He got this mutated in own name after submitting the affidavit and the application. In the voter list of Assembly Election of 1995 and 1998, the name stood recorded at Sr. no. 186 which was subsequently rectified as Kamala Nihora due to wrongful entry in the list of 1995. In 1996, Election Commission issued the Identity Card No.402105 in the name of respondent no.1 which was mentioned in the voter list also.

36. Makkhanlal PW3 has supported the fact of succession of respondent no.1 upon the seat after the death of Nihora and accrual of property and K.L. Pandey PW4 has supported mutation of building no. 124 in favour of Kamala Nihora through an application and affidavit, Vishwadarshan Gaur PW5 has supported Kamendra Singh on the fact of publication of news in the issue dated 12.09.1993 of the daily *"Dainik Madhya Pradesh"* about succession of respondent no.1 Kamala Nihora

to the seat of *guru* as per *panch nirnaya.* His statement stand corroborated with Assembly voter list,1995, 1998, amended list Ex.P/7,8 and 9, Voter's ID Card Ex.P/10, Mutation application, affidavit, statement (on Note Sheet), notification, *panch nirnaya* Ex. P/16 to Ex. P/20 of the register entries and Ex. P/21 news paper "*Dainik Madhya Pradesh*".

37. Joint Branch Manager, Bank of Baroda, Branch Katni Shri R.S. Dahiya DW/2 (respondent no. 3) states that Kamala Khan eunuch @ Kamaluddin had opened Saving Bank Account no. 3440 in his bank by submitting an application with thumb impression as being illiterate on the identification by Ravitra Katoti. Subsequently, after learning to sign, cheque book was issued in the same S.B. Account on 10.08.1991. In the cross examination, this witness is not contradicted and respondent no. 1 Kamala admitted in own statement in para no. 43 that at the time of opening bank account, thumb impression was affixed but subsequently signatures were put.

38. The petitioner Kamendra Singh states in Para no.8 that in issue dated 12.09.1993 of "*Dainik Madhya Pradesh*", photograph of respondent no.1 was published along with the news item of dispute amongst the eunuch community and about *panch nirnaya.* He states in para no. 14 that Election Commission had issued an ID Card No. 402105 Ex.P/10 along with photograph of the respondent. Vishwadarshan Gaur PW/5 states that the photo published in Ex. P/21 is that of present Mayor. R.S. Dahiya DW/2 (respondent no.3) stated that on the application for opening account Ex.D/3, photographs of Kamala @ Kamaluddin is pasted and the same person is the mayor of Katni at present.

39. Respondent has not directly refuted any of the facts. It means that the respondent has not denied the affixture of photograph on these documents. The more important fact is that respondent no. 1 has produced own Passport Ex. D/3 and it has been admitted in para

no. 42 that "the said Passport bears my photograph". On 31.08.2000 i.e. after 7 months from the date of presentation of the petition, the photograph of the respondent no.1 which is affixed on the Passport prepared voluntarily completely match with that of Ex.P/10, Ex.P/21 and Ex.D/3 (application for opening an account).

40. In addition to the aforesaid facts, it is also clear from the physical appearance of the respondent no.1 in different national festivals like Independence Day, Republic Day, etc. and publication of the photograph of the respondent no.1 during the last 2½ years in all the magazines, journals and television, that photographs affixed on Ex.P/10, P/21 and Ex.D/3 are of the respondent no.1 only. Thus, the bank account and photographs also fully corroborate the statements of the petitioner.

41. Respondent no.1 has described as having no concern with the Assembly voting list, Nihora, its assets like building, *guru* seat and its disputes. In the statements recorded, respondent no.1 states that "I do not know Haji Jumman or Nihora, I have nothing to do with them, and I have never submitted any application in the Municipal Corporation for mutation of the house where I am living nor has submitted any affidavit. I do not know anything about the *gaddi* (seat). I do not know even about any dispute regarding the Seat." In para no. 5, respondent no.1 states "While recording my name in the voter list, I did not ask to write my name as Kamala, parenthood Nihora. I do not know Kamala, parenthood Nihora. No person of this name has ever resided in my locality." However, during the cross examination, the witness could not conceal this ignorance.

42. Kamala Bai DW/1 stated in para no. 12, 17, 21 and 28 that she had come to stay in Katni about 30-40 years back and since then she has been living in the house of eunuchs in their locality in Alfertganj situated near the

house of Ayaz Khan. She has replied evasively on the questions of titles or ownership over the said house. She stated that she did not purchase the house and is paying the rent thereof but however, again stated that she could not tell as to whom (eunuch) she pays the rent. She does not have any receipt of the rent. About the rent amount, she states that it is about Rs. 20 or Rs. 25 per month. She states that she does not know as to who is the owner of the house and, therefore, has not made any payment of rent to anybody. In para no. 22 and 23, she states that after being appointed as Mayor, she never attempted to search as to in whose name was the records of the house. Despite all these things, she admitted that she repairs the entire house. She further states that electric and water meter are not in her name but she pays the bills. She deposits tax of the house also in the Municipal Corporation.

43. The respondent has produced Kamala Nihora in evidence despite being unknown to her. Kamala Nihora (DW/6, respondent no. 1) has stated that Nihora was their *guru*. Guru has bequeathed the seat 9 years back to the respondent. House of the *Guru* stands recorded in the name of the respondent. In that house, the disciple eunuchs are living, respondent does not claim any rent from them. The respondent further states that Kamala Mausi (respondent no. 1) used to live with the respondent in the same house and she used to prepare food etc. but does not know as to whom are the other eunuchs residing there. In this way, the witness has rebutted the facts stated by the respondent Kamala Bai.

44. Respondent has admitted in para no. 23 that Demand Notes of the Municipal Corporation for tax of the house are not received in the name (Kamala, parenthood unknown). It is admitted in para no. 22 that bills of water/electricity of the house are received in the name of Kamala @ Kamaluddin.

45. Kamala Bai DW/1 states in para No. 23 that she has

never seen Kamala @ Kamaluddin. In para No.22 she states that she does not know whether the house, in which she is living, is in the name of Kamala @ Kamaluddin, whereas Abdul Kuddus DW/4 (respondent no. 1) states in para No. 5 (?) the house of Kamala Mausi is in fact in the name of Kamala @ Kamaluddin.

46. The respondent states in para no. 21 that the place where she is living is the house and not the inn of eunuchs but in para no. 22 she states that there are 5-6 rooms in the house. She lives in one room. In other rooms, eunuchs are living. Kamala Nihora DW/6 states that the house in which Kamala Mausi lives, some disciple eunuchs are also living. Abdul Kuddus DW/4 - respondent no.1 states in para no. 5 that the place where Kamala Mausi lives from before is an inn for the eunuchs. All the eunuchs of Katni stay there.

47. Respondent Kamala Bai states that she does not know Kamala Nihora but Kamala Nihora DW/6 states that Kamala Mausi lives along with the DW/6. In the voter list of Municipal Corporation of 1999 which has been relied upon by the respondent herself, the resident of Kamala Nihora at Sr. no. 643 and Kamala unknown at Sr.no. 644 is shown at the same place House no. 124. K.L. Pandey PW/4, who is Revenue Officer in the Municipal Corporation, states that name of Kamala Jaan, parenthood Nihora stands recorded in the records of Corporation over the House no. 124. There is no other entry in the name of Kamala Jaan, parenthood unknown in the 10 houses over and below the said house.

48. Respondent Kamala Bai though has stated that she is not known to Jumman and Nihora, but her neighbour tailor Ghasiram DW/5 states in para no. 6 that in Subhash Ward there used to live one eunuch named Jumman. After expressing ignorance about *guru* of the eunuchs, the witness admits that after the death of Jumman, Nihora was elected *guru* of the

eunuchs. The respondent herself admitted in para no. 33 that after the death of eunuchs' *guru*, his disciple takes over. Obviously, Nihora took over after the death of Jumman who himself was the *guru* of the eunuchs.

49. Ghasiram (DW/5, respondent no. 1) states that after the death of Nihora, there is no *guru*. Nihora died in the year 1993. For the last 9-10 years, there is no *guru* of eunuchs. It is not natural. The witness has attempted to conceal facts but Tara Bai and Angoori Bai have clarified the position.
50. Angoori Bai (DW/2, respondent no. 1) states in para no.7 that after the death of Nihora, his entire work is looked after by Kamala Jaan. Respondent Kamala Bai states in para no. 32 that before being appointed as Mayor, she was known as Kamala Jaan. Angoori Bai states that after the demise of Nihora, Kamala Jaan is taking care of eunuchs in Katni. Kamala, parenthood Nihora DW/6 respondent no.1 states in para no. 10 that in the eunuch community, their care is taken by the *guru*. Angoori Bai states in para no. 7 that after Nihora, the respondent no. 1 is taking care of her house. According to the respondent, after the death of *guru*, the assets are inherited to the disciple. Therefore, inheritance of Nihora's house in respondent's favour is clear.
51. Angoori Bai has not straight away regarded respondent Kamala as *guru* of the eunuchs but after beating about the bush, she admits. But Tara Bai (DW/1, respondent no.1) has fully clarified this ambiguity. In para no.1, she described the respondent as her daughter and in the last lines of para no. 4, clarified that her daughter was the *guru* in Katni and the same is Mayor today.
52. Respondent states that there were several errors in the Voter Identity Cards. Names, parenthood and photographs were wrongly recorded or affixed. That is why, these cards have not been used since then in any of the elections. The news paper has no validity in

the eyes of evidence. The original notification has not been produced. The voter list of the Assembly has no application in the elections of Municipal Corporation. At the time of opening Bank Account, the name was recorded as Kamal and nothing else was recorded. The application must have been filled up by the bank people. She does not know Ravitra Katoti.

53. It is true that at the time of preparing voters' Identity Cards, some errors were committed e.g. respondent counsel Ayaz Khan has disclosed one error in the ID Card of his wife but on the basis of the apprehension or possibility, it cannot be inferred that all the identity cards were full of errors. It has not been proved as to what was the specific error in Ex. P/10 ID Card. It has been argued that in that card, against the name of Kamala, parenthood Nihora, the photographs of the respondent was affixed by mistake but against that, no action has so far taken till date, there is no argument or evidence to this effect. In all these 7 years, votes have been cast in several elections but there appears no attempt to rectify the mistake and, therefore, after seven years and particularly after presentation of the petition, the respondent's contention is not liable to be accepted.
54. The said ID Cards were not used in the election not because they were full of errors but because the process of preparing ID Cards for all the voters could not be completed for different reasons. Therefore, this argument of the respondent is not worth accepting.
55. It is true that Vishwadarshan Gaur PW/5 has admitted that notice for publication which they get, are duly inquired upon. The notice of Ex. P/21 was published without any inquiry as it was received. There is no record available in the office as to from where, the said notice was received and as to who presented it in the office. But the witness states that notices are published as they are by them on the basis of belief. In cases of any mistakes or errors, they publish corrigendum. There is no evidence of any such corrigendum

regarding Ex. P/21. According to the witness, the record of the *panch* decision or the notices is preserved for 2 years and thereafter destroyed. The incident dates back to 7 years and, therefore, he does not remember as to from where the notice was received.

56. Witness Vishwadarshan Gaur does admit that anything may be published at any time in the printing press but he states that newspaper cannot be published like this. He has admitted that any newspaper may be printed in other printing press but from the quality of paper used, it can be gathered whether the newspaper is old one or a fresh. Thus, the witness has duly disposed off all the suspicions/doubts raised by the respondent, therefore, the evidence value of his statement and Ex.P/21 newspaper which was published well before the present dispute in the ordinary course of business without any prior intention is not decimated.

57. The respondent states that petitioner has not pleaded regarding mutation order or publication in the newspaper. Such fact which is out side the pleadings cannot be admitted as evidence. But these documents are not "relevant fact or issues". But is the evidence, adduced to prove the fact on issue. As per Order 5 Rule 2 Sub Rule 1 of the CPC, the pleadings should contain short description of only those relevant facts which the party relies upon for the claim or defence. Such evidence shall not be described from which those facts are proved. According to this legal provision, the respondent's stand is immaterial.

58. R.S. Dahiya (DW/2, respondent no. 3) admits that account of Ex. D/3 was not opened in his presence. The account holder did not affix thumb impression before him (para 14). The process of account opening was not conducted before him (para 18). The account holder never appeared before him for withdrawal (para 19). He had seen the present Mayor sitting on a motorcycle along with someone and at that time, somebody had pointed out that the person is Mayor. But none of these

adversely affects the validity of Ex. D/3 (Application for SB Account).

59. Ex. D/3 was prepared in the ordinary course of business in the office of public sector undertaking bank. This has been produced by the Joint Branch Manager from his due custody who enjoys the lawful custody over such documents being a responsible officer. This was created long before the present dispute without any prejudice. The respondent has not denied thumb impression, signature or photograph upon the said document and what is more important is that the respondent herself admitted its existence. Its veracity has not been assailed. The photograph affixed on the said document discards all the arguments of the respondent.

60. The voter lists of the Assembly are stated to be inconsistent with this case and inadmissible in the evidence but these lists are relevant to the facts reported by the petitioner and to the issues of the case. No objection has been raised at the time of their admissibility. As per the citation **AIR 1991 Orissa 166 (Naladhar Mahapatra and another Vs. Seva Dibya and others)**, after admitting of a document, without there being any objection, the same cannot be questioned at later stage. According to the said citation, the voter list is a public document. It does not require any formal verification. Its certified copy is admissible in evidence under Section 77 of the Evidence Act; therefore, the objection of the respondent is baseless.

61. In order to show that respondent no.1 is not Kamala, parenthood Nihora, he has examined a witness named Kamala, parenthood Nihora (DW/6, respondent no. 1). This witness stated that she lived in Katni for 30-40 years and for the last 4-5 years, she is not living there. Her *guru* was Nihora. About 9 years back, he died and handed over his seat to her. House of the *guru* stands recorded in the record of Municipal Corporation in her name. Kamala Mausi came to Katni from Gwalior after

a year from her elevation as *guru*. But the statement of this witness is contradictory and full of infirmities.

62. The witness (Kamala, parenthood Nihora DW/6) stated in para no. 1 that she lived in Katni for 30-40 years and is not living for the last 4-5 years, which means she had come to Katni about 45 years back but in para no. 4, it is stated that she had come to Katni 15 years before the death of Nihora. She states in para no. 1 that Nihora died 9 years back which means that she had come to Katni about 24-25 years back. In para no. 1, she states that she is not living in Katni for the last 4-5 years. Further states in para no. 4 that she lived in Katni for 8-9 years after the death of Nihora. She has admitted that Nihora died about 9 years back which means that she was in the Katni till then.
63. It is stated in para no. 13 that each eunuch knows the *guru*. But in para no. 4, it is stated that she does not know the *guru* of Banda whereas in para no. 13, every eunuch knows the name of *guru*. As per para no. 11, she does not know the *gurus* of Kamore, Sleemanabad, Satna, Maiher, Sagar and Shahdol. This witness does not know her ward, counsellor and the residents. She has no knowledge of the geographical location around her house. She does not know anything about Katni. She has stated about the statue of Subhashji at the main square in place of Nehruji. She does not know anything about the eunuch community in Katni. She has forgotten her telephone number. She does not remember number of the house or the amount of tax. She does not have any ration card or bank account here, whereas, as per the respondent, she has the account. She does not know the disciple eunuchs reported as per *panch* decision *viz*. Jyoti, Sunita and Bahar Rani. She does not know anything about the death of eunuch Asha as per *panch* decision took place about a year back. She never acted as *guru* in Banda after taking over the seat here. No respondent witness has stated about the

existence of this witness. Therefore, this witness is not at all credible.

64. Angoori Bai has given testimony about bringing up the respondent as she was orphan but in para no. 4 it is stated that about one year back, after her election as Mayor, she met her at *Bada* (Gwalior) when Kamala Bai was accorded a warm welcome.

65. If the claim of the respondent (no. 1) is tested in order to ascertain whether he is Kamala, parenthood unknown, the respondent states in this regard that she was born in Banda. Tara Bai and Angoori Bai state that they got her as orphan in Banda. They took her to Gwalior. They brought her up. Thereafter, she started living in Katni. Respondent states in para no. 2 and 4 that her name was recorded in the voter list of the last Municipal Election. Abdul Kuddus (DW/4, respondent no. 1) and Ghasiram (DW/5, respondent no. 1) have corroborated her. Abdul Kuddus has proved the voter list (Ex. D/2) of the Municipal Election for the year 1999. In Sr. no. 644 of that list, it is recorded as Kamala, parenthood unknown. This all is the evidence which has been adduced by the respondent.

66. The respondent has also seriously argued on this point that in the voter list of Municipal Election of 1994, her name was recorded as Kamala, parenthood unknown. As per Election Rules, 1994, no objection was raised against this list. On that basis alone, her name was recorded at Sr. no. 644 of the voter list of 1999. No appeal was even preferred as per Rule 9 against that. No objection of any kind was taken and, therefore, the present petition is not maintainable. Witness Kamendra Singh has admitted that no objection was raised about the voter list of 1999.

67. Upon appreciation of evidence of the respondent, it follows that the testimony is contradictory and full of infirmities. Petitioner Kamendra Singh was suggested in para no. 68 of his cross-examination that respondent no. 1 happened to be found to the eunuchs as a newly

born child. Tara Bai states that they found her as newly born female baby. At that time, her age must have been 1½ years. According to Tara Bai, she got the child and she brought her up. Angoori Bai is right in stating that her Munni Bai (elder to mother) got her and she brought her up. Information of the orphan child was given at the police station but there is no evidence and the verbal statement is full of infirmities, unnatural and incredible. Tara or Munni states that they brought up the newly born baby for 15-20 years. Experience says that nobody has ever seen any minor child or baby till date with the eunuchs.

68. Kamala, parenthood Nihora DW/6 states against these witnesses that she was brought by Sitara eunuch from Gwalior to Katni and not by Tara, Munni and Angoori. According to Tara Bai, the respondent herself had come to Katni at the age of 15-16 years and according to Angoori Bai, she was of 24-25 years of age at that time.

69. The story of respondent that she was brought up by Angoori Bai and Tara Bai as a newly born baby and was brought from Banda to Gwalior and then to Katni stands rebutted by the affidavit Ex.P/14 of the respondent. This does not contain any fact about the respondent having been brought up in Gwalior. There is no story about bringing her from Gwalior to Katni. It only mentions that after her birth, she lived in Banda for 15-16 years and then came to Kamore and has been living in Subhash ward, Katni for 20 years. Therefore, the entire evidence of Angoori Bai and Tara Bai is an after-thought and not credible.

70. According to Tara Bai, Kamala lived with her for about 15 years and then started living in Katni on the ground that she would take care of herself. Angoori Bai states that she lived with her for 20-25 years and she brought her up then shifted to Katni. Kamala Bai (respondent) herself stated that she had come to Katni about 30-40 years back and since then has been living in Katni in a house. Tara Bai states that she did not lodge any report

in the police station when she found Kamala. According to her, the police personnel asked her when she is willing to bring her up what is the need of lodging the report. This statement is not believable. Evidence is not on record that Angoori Bai's elder mother Munni Bai somehow lodged information in the police station. Angoori states in para no. 4 that she met her (respondent) in a welcome ceremony one year after her election as Mayor. According to both the witnesses, she lives in Gwalior. Their statements are unbelievable as to for what and for whom and when she came from Banda.

71. The witnesses Abdul Kuddus and Ghasiram (DW/4 and DW/5 respondent no.1) have stated about adding the name of the respondent in the voter list of 1994 but the respondent has not stated like this. She has only stated in para no.2 and 4 that her name was recorded in the voter list of the last Municipal Election. Abdul Kuddus and Ghasiram have simultaneously stated about addition of names of 10-12 persons but have not stated about any information of those persons. Voter list of the 1994 has neither been produced nor verified and, therefore, the arguments in this regard become immaterial.

72. In the voter list of 1999, Kamala Nihora and Kamala unknown are mentioned to be living at the same place. Kamala Nihora (DW/6, respondent no. 1) states in para no. 3 that Kamala Mausi (respondent) lived in her house. She used to prepare food. However, Kamala Jaan respondent states *suo motu* that she does not know Kamala Nihora or Kamala @ Kamaluddin. She has never seen them and even did not live with them. Kamala Bai (respondent) states that she has been living in Katni for the last 30-40 years but has not produced for verification, any of the Government records naturally required during such a long span like Ration Card, Voter List, Bills of water/electricity, rent note of the house, title deeds or Corporation tax documents.

73. In the year 1994 and 1998, voter list for the Assembly election were prepared but surprisingly the name of Kamala Nihora residing in the same house finds place and rectified too due to typographical mistake but name of Kamala unknown does not find place whereas the respondent herself states that she has been living in Katni for the last 30-40 years and, therefore, the entry in the list of Municipal Corporation prepared at the local level becomes doubtful.
74. It would be worthwhile to mention here that in the voter list of 1999, if name of Kamala unknown was written, the same is a written entry recorded on the basis of a prayer of self. As per Section 21 of the Evidence Act, admissions cannot be proved by or on behalf of the person who makes them. In this regard, the citation of **Idandas Vs. Anant Ramchandra Phadke (Dead) by LRS 1982 (1) SCC 27** is worth perusing. Section 21 of the Evidence Act and the provisions envisaged therein do not have application in the present case as the circumstances do not exist.
75. From another point of view, entry of Kamala, unknown parenthood in the voter list is dubious. In the voter list of 1994, the age of Kamala, unknown parenthood, is recorded as 45 years and in the list of 1999 Ex/D/2, her age is recorded 45 years even after lapse of 4 years. Even in the affidavit dated 02.12.1999—sworn in before the election, the age is recorded as 45 years. If the name is repeated in the list of 1999 from the list of 1994, the changes in the age must have been naturally incorporated. With regard to change in age, the respondent has produced the directions issued by the Central Government along with the written arguments, in Schedule-F of the directions, in which it is mentioned that the change in age should be incorporated "necessarily". But failure to incorporate changes like this, create doubts against the entry in the list.
76. It is clear from the appreciation and analysis of all the evidence, those statements of petitioner Kamendra

Singh stands well corroborated by the non-rebuttal of the statement of petitioner's witnesses in cross-examination and even stands corroborated by the respondent's witnesses themselves and even by the Bank account, Election ID Card, voter list and mutation etc. Bare perusal of the evidence makes it evident that respondent no.1 herself is not Kamala, parenthood unknown, but is Kamala, parenthood Nihora, as Kamala alone succeeded to the *guru-gaddi* after the death of Nihora and inherited the *guru's* property as per traditions of the eunuch community. Before the suit elections, Kamala was the *guru* of the eunuchs in Katni and is at present too. Kamala has got mutated the Nihora's house in her own name and opened account in the bank and even operated it, Kamala's name was recorded in the voter list of Assembly Election and was issued with the Voter's ID Card. The version of Kamala, parenthood unknown, was fabricated before the suit election. The same story was advanced through the testimony of Angoori Bai and Tara Bai and contradicting evidence was produced through them against her pleadings and the affidavit, therefore, the same cannot be relied upon.

77. The petitioners have stated that respondent no.1 Kamala Nihora is a eunuch whereas, the respondent states that she was born as a female child and she is a woman. She started living with the eunuchs because she was brought by them and out of this affection; she had adopted the nickname of eunuch.

78. It is clear from the evidence of both parties in this regard that petitioner Kamendra Singh has described her as eunuch but has not stated any special ground for the same. He has stated the same only from physical appearance but admitted that he has not attended any convention of the eunuchs. He has no special information about the eunuchs. He never happened to visit Subhash ward. He had not seen the respondent before the election. During the elections, he described

the respondent as male or eunuch on the basis of his physical appearance. Makkhanlal PW/3 states that at one occasion, the respondent lifted the *saree* before him and he saw that he was a male person. But this statement of the witness is not natural. The witness has stated that he had seen the respondent going for *namaz* in the mosque of Alfertganj but in the detailed cross-examination, it becomes clear that in the circumstances of mosque and under the circumstances in which the witnesses saw the respondent, it is not credible. But this position does not adversely affect the version of the petitioner.

79. As already stated in para no. 34 that the respondent did refute that she is not Kamala Nihora but it was not specifically refuted that Kamala Nihora was a eunuch.

80. Kamendra Singh has stated that Nihora, *guru* of eunuchs died in the year 1993 and thereafter, the respondent took over as *guru*. News to this effect was published in the newspaper. Makkhanlal has supported this version. Vishwadarshan Gaur has corroborated publication of news item. According to Kamendra Singh, Nihora's house succeeded in favour of the respondent which the respondent got mutated in own name. This fact is proved from the statements of K.L. Pandey PW/4, record of mutation registers and *panchnama* applications, etc. The respondent has denied having any relation with Nihora or from describing herself as *guru* of eunuchs but in cross-examination, respondent has indirectly admitted that he has been living in the house of Nihora right from the beginning, used to repair it, make payment of water/electricity bills and pay the tax to Municipal Corporation. DW Angoori Bai has stated that formerly *Haji* Jumman was the *guru* of eunuchs in Katni, after the death of Jumman, Nihora succeeded. But the witness has tried to conceal as to who succeed after the death of Nihora but has admitted that after the death of Nihora, the respondent is looking after his entire work. She has been taking care of the

house. Tara Bai DW/1 has admitted in her examination without any suggestion that after the death of Nihora her daughter i.e. respondent no. 1 has become the *guru* of eunuchs. *Guru* of eunuchs is the same person who is at present holding the post of Mayor. DW/1 Tara Bai states that she herself is a eunuch and they do not let any other person to join their community except the eunuchs. They do not allow any other person except eunuchs to hold the position in their community. The respondent has tried to describe herself as barren lady but she has clearly stated that barren woman is not called eunuch. The respondent has admitted in para No.16 that she never had a desire for sexual intercourse. Her statement regarding usual bodily process of women also is not credible.

81. DW/1 Tara Bai states that she herself is a eunuch and they do not let any other person to join their community except eunuchs. They do not allow any other person except eunuchs to hold the position in their community. The respondent has tried to describe herself as barren lady but she has clearly stated that a barren woman is not called eunuch. The respondent has admitted in para no.16 that she never had a desire for sexual intercourse. Her statement regarding usual biological process of women also is not credible.

82. At all the places, "eunuch" is suffixed to the name of the respondent. The respondent has tried to explain that she is not a eunuch but due to the fact of being brought up by the eunuchs, she has adopted the nickname "eunuch" out of affection. She has tried to explain citing several examples that no person turns to be the other one merely by virtue of adoption of nickname e.g. no person becomes mad merely by virtue of adopting the nickname *pagal*. But here also, this is a futile attempt by the respondent to conceal originality.

83. There is no past record of the life of respondent stated to be spent in Banda, Gwalior or Kamore. The first ever record available pertains to Katni after the death of

Nihora *guru*. The use of word "eunuch" as nickname of the respondent does not find place in the *panch* decision delivered on succession after the death of Nihora on 04.04.1993 (appended to the mutation register) and in the statement dated 02.04.1993 recorded on Note Sheet of the mutation register. Again, there is no mention of any nickname or "eunuch" suffixed to the name of respondent in the application for mutation Ex. P/17 and the affidavit dated 12.04.1993 Ex. P/18. The same is the case with Ex.P/21. In the bank account Ex. D/3, the word "eunuch" is not mentioned. There is no document like ration card. And even more, in the entry no. 644 in voter list Ex. D/2 which is relied upon by the respondent herself, the nickname does not find place. In the affidavit Ex. P/14 submitted before the election (submitted along with the nomination form) the word eunuch does not find place in any form, what to speak of a nickname. In the nomination form, the word eunuch does find place but it is not intended to mean nickname. In the passport Ex. D/3 prepared voluntarily seven months after the election, the nickname does not find place. All these facts go to show that the respondent never used the word "eunuch" as his nickname much before the beginning of the elections till quite a long time after the elections. This defence was artificially created only in the written statement and was never resorted to in the past nor in the future, therefore, is it clear that eunuch is not a nickname of respondent no.1 but he himself is a eunuch.

84. Now the question is whether the eunuchs are males or females? In this regard, reference of our old religious epics are worthy to state and we find that from time immemorial, the reference of eunuchs finds place in many religious and historical stories. In *Satapatha Brahmanav,* v.i.2.14,iv.1,1; In *Atharvaveda,* vi.cxxxviii.2; *Mahabharata,* v.clx.115, mention of eunuchs and long haired persons who were neither males nor females

finds place. In *Manu Smriti* also, persons who are neither males nor females have been described as impotent and provisions have been made depriving them of any rights in succession.

85. According to Hindu mythology, during the period of exile of Lord Rama, the eunuchs too accompanied the Ayodhya residents to see off Lord Rama at the edge of the forest, Lord Rama directed all the males and females to go back but for want of specific orders to them for returning, they waited for Lord Rama for 14 years and sought blessings of Lord Rama only after his return after Lanka Victory.
86. In the religious epic *Mahabharata*, the instances of renowned and popular impotent or eunuchs like Shikhandi and Vrihannala find a mention which have become acronym for the impotent and eunuchs. During the period of exile, Arjuna himself who was a great warrior (male) acted as eunuch Vrihannala, music teacher as a sequel to a curse in Viraat Nagar to teach musical skills to princess Uttara, daughter of King Viraat. In the later years, when the Kauravas took away the cattle of Viraat Nagar, Vrihannala the eunuch drove the chariot of prince Uttar as the driver in the battle ground and when the prince was frightened, Vrihannala himself took the reins of battle and defeated the Kauravas Army. Shikhandi, the son of King Dhrupad was also a male eunuch and drove the chariot. In the world renowned *Mahabharata* battle, he became the cause of death of great warrior and Chief Commander Bhisma Pitamaha of Pandavas' Army.
87. In the Chapter-ix of *Samprayogikam Dwitiyamadhikaranam* of Kama Sutra authored by Maharishi Vatsyayana, it is mentioned in *sutra*-1 of *Auparishtaka Prakaran* "Dwividha tratiyaprakratiah strirupini purushrupini cha" (*Tratiya* is of two kinds, one is female and another is male). Further it is stated that
"Tratiyaprakritinarpunsakam strirupini strisansthana stanadiyogat. Purushrupini purushsansthana

ramastulomadiyogat yadyadattimani - pyoprisht kamanyostadwachyate"

(*Tratiya prakriti* is called impotent, body of one resembles that of a female i.e. has breast, etc. whereas the body of other one has beard-mustache etc. Livelihood of both of them is called *auparishtaka vidhaan* and they are treated accordingly).

88. The *jaghan karma* of the mouth is called *auparishtaka,* according to the aforesaid epic, the impotent resembling the female is called *kleeve.* Description of different activities of both these forms of *tratiya* (impotent) is given in *sutra* no.24 of Chapter-ix.
89. In *sutra* no. 5 of Chapter-xvi of *Paridarikam Panchamadhikaranam* of Kama Sutra, it is stated that "Striyogenav Purushanamadhya labdhavrattinam viyonishu vijatishu stripratimasu kevalopmardanachabhi prayanivittirvyakhyata".

    (Such uses of females satisfy the intentions of those males who do not get females, and are also depicted for barren ones, in alien castes in female structures and in *updharman*).
90. It has been further stated in the *sutras* that as the intentions of female are naturally met in the male turned females, similar is the position with males.
91. Instances of appointing eunuchs in Royal Courts (Rajdarbar) finds place between 2nd to 5th centuries. Description of eunuchs acting as male or female under the concealed pretext of male or female also find place. Eunuchs resembling female used to live in the capacity of chamberlain of internal part of Royal Court and satisfy their sexual desires by way of oral sex. Eunuchs resembling males used to serve as chamberlain in the outer parts.
92. In the medieval times of Indian history, there are several instances of eunuchs e.g. the commanders Ullugh Khan and Nusrat Khan of founder of Khilji dynasty. Ala-ud-din Khilji found a eunuch named Kafur *khoja* during the Gujarat victory in 1299 A.D., who was subsequently

promoted as Commander named Malik Kafur. During the last phase of Tughlaq dynasty from 1388-1414 A.D., when the State of Delhi was destroyed, Malik Sarwar who got the title of Sultan-ush-Sharq, became the independent ruler of Jaunpur and laid the foundation of 'the Sharqi Kingdom'. Malik Sarwar was also a eunuch. Several instances of appointing eunuchs as harem attendants are found in Mughal dynasty. In 1603 A.D. also, one instance is on record when Saleem son of Akbar made one of his servants an impotent. Due to the traditions of the Mughal dynasty only, the eunuchs were known as harem attendants.

93. Right from the beginning of Muslim religion, the reference of eunuchs finds place. In the book titled *Mishkat al-Masabih* by Dr. A.N. Matthews, it is found that at one occasion, Uthman Ibn Majun sought permission from Prophet Mohammed for castration which was refused being against the religion and it was directed that whosoever castrates himself or other's cannot be his followers. Instances of accepting by Prophet Mohammed, those who voluntarily became eunuchs are also found. The Christians and the Jews used to adopt the process of making impotent outside *Darr-ul-Islam* which was subsequently adopted by the Islam. According to Ayalon, 1977:270-271, during the reign of Ibn Batuta of Mamluk Sultanate, Abyssinians or eunuchs of other caste were kept as attendant or chamberlain for the protection of the mosque al-Madina under the directions of the chief eunuch (Shaykh al-Khuddam).

94. In Christianity, it did not get any formal recognition from the Church but in the early days of the history, for observance of religious celibacy, the tradition of voluntary castration is noticed which was prevalent predominantly in the 3rd century. Between the 16th and 18th centuries, the female singers were prohibited to sing in the Roman Catholic Church, therefore, boys with soprano voice were castrated into eunuch so that

they could join the chorus in the Church. Such boys, who were castrated for voice, were called castrati. Carlo Broschi (1705-82) was famous Italian castrati. This tradition had gained much popularity in Italy before the interception by Pope Leo XIII in 1878.

95. Instances of China and Middle East have been dealt at the time of defining word "Eunuch".
96. In all the religious and historical instances as aforesaid, the fact of eunuch being only a male person is revealed.
97. In several dictionaries and encyclopedias also, the word eunuch has been referred and the same is stated below:-
    (i) *Oxford Dictionary* - Eunuch means - A castrated man especially one formally employed at an Oriental court or harem.
    (ii) *Bhargava's Dictionary* - Eunuch means - A castrated male person.
    (iii) *Webster's II New Riverside University Dictionary*—Eunuch means—
        (1) A castrated man employed as a harem attendant or functionary in certain Oriental courts.
        (2) A man with undeveloped testes.
    (iv) *Penguin Dictionary*—Eunuch means—
        (1) A castrated man employed as a guard in a harem or as a chamberlain in a palace.
        (2) A man or boy deprived of testes or external genitals.
        (3) A man lacking effectiveness or vitality.
98. As per the different Encyclopedias:
    (i) *Encyclopedia Britannica* (Vol. VIII, 1965): eunuchs are castrated men.
    (ii) *Encarta Enyclopedia*: Eunuch–Castrated human male. From ancient times, in the far and middle East, eunuchs were used to take charge of the women in harems or to serve as chamberlains. They often attained positions of great influence, and in Egypt the term was applied to any court officer whether or not he had undergone castration.

The Idea that eunuchs were lacking in courage and intelligence is refuted by the histories of Iran, India and China, where they were active and effective in public affairs. The employment of eunuchs reached its height in the courts of the Byzantine Empire.

Boys who were castrated in order to keep their soprano voices were known as Castrati, the Italian Soprano Carlo Broschi widespread in Italy until the accession of Pope Leo XIII in 1878. The voluntary practice of castration for religious celibacy appeared early in Christian History and was most prevalent in the 3rd century, but it was never officially approved by the Church and came to be violently denounced.

(iii) *Oxford Encyclopedia*: Eunuch–a castrated human male. Eunuchs were used as guardians of harem in ancient China and in Persian Empire of the Achaemenids and also at the courts of the Byzantine Emperors and the Ottoman Sultans. They became the friends and advisors of the Rulers of these powers, as they did of Roman Emperors.

Castration was also imposed as a form of punishment (Abelard suffered in this way); was practiced voluntarily by some Christian sects (the most notable Christian eunuch being the theologian Origin); and was used to produce male adult sopranos in Italy—castrati—until Pope Leo XIII banned the practice in 1878.

(iv) *Comptons Encyclopedia*: Eunuch—The later Han period was particularly plagued with evils caused by eunuchs, castrated males recruited from the lower classes to serve as bodyguards for the Imperial Harem. Coming from the uneducated and poor backgrounds they were ruthlessly ambitious once they were placed within reach of power. Towards the end of later Han, power struggles between the eunuchs and the landlords—officials were prolonged and destructive peasant rebellions of the Taoist—leaning Yellow Turbans in 184 and five lack of Rice in 190 led to the rise of generals who massacred over 2,000 eunuchs, destroyed the capital, and one after another became Dictators.

(v) *New Millenium Encyclopedia*: Eunuch—Castrated Human Male. From the ancient times, in the far and middle East, eunuchs were used to take charge of women in harems or to serve as chamberlains. They often attained positions of great influence, and in Egypt the term was applied to any court officer whether or not he was castrated. The idea that eunuchs were lacking in courage and intelligence is refuted by the histories of Iran, India and China, where they were active and effective in public affairs. The employment of eunuchs reached its height in the courts of the Byzantine Emperors at Constantinople. Muslim rulers employed eunuchs mainly as harem officials.

Boys who were castrated in order to keep their soprano voices were known as castrati; the Italian Soprano Carlo Broschi Farinelli (1705-82) was one of the famous castrati ....

(vi) *The Hutchinson Encyclopedia*: Eunuch—a castrated man. Originally eunuchs were simply bedchamber attendants in harems in the East (*eunoukhos* is a Greek word for 'one in charge of a bed') but as they were usually castrated so that they should not take too great an interest in their charges, the term applied more generally. Eunuchs often filled high offices of State in China, India and Persia. Italian castrati were singers castrated as boys to preserve their high voices, a practice which ceased on the accession of Pope Leo XIII in 1878.

99. Thus, in different dictionaries and encyclopedias, 'eunuch' is described as "castrated man". From the perusal of the word 'castration' in dictionaries, encyclopedias etc., it is clear that it means that removing gonads, gelding and process of impotency.

100. According to *Readers Digest Dictionary*—castrate, geld, emasculate, Neuter Castrated male chicken fattened for eating CAPON, Castrated male horse or other animal GELDING—Castrated male sheep WHETHER, Castrated man, especially in former times, serving as a harem guard, court attendant or like the eunuch, Pig castrated before reaching maturity BORROW pig or other animal castrated after maturity--STAG.
101. According to *New Millennium Encyclopedia*—Castration-removal of gonads in human or animal–In Animal Husbandry–castration of male animals is called gelding.
102. Accordingly to *Encarta Encyclopedia*—Castration means removal of gonads (testes in men, ovaries in women) in human beings or animals. And it has been defined in the same way in the other dictionaries and encyclopedias mentioned above.
103. In order to get real meaning of word eunuch, I have studied the following books—*Medical Jurisprudence and Toxicology* by Dr. S.S. Daniel and D.K. Tiwari; *Medical Jurisprudence* and *Toxicology* by Dr. Parikh, *Medical Jurisprudence* and *Toxicology* by Rajaram Yadav. Text Book of *Medical Jurisprudence and Toxicology* (1980) by Shri Modi, *Medical Jurisprudence and Toxicology* by Shri K.K. Singh. At Page No. 435 of his book Dr. Daniel states that among human beings, is found a species which is neither male nor female but is a composite form of both the genders. Such persons are called male prostitute or eunuch. Tradition of sodomy is mostly found in such species. They have got breast but no vagina. From physical appearance, they look like a woman, keep hairs and dress up like a woman.
104. Shri Modi has also opined the like observations at Page no. 347 of his book, 'Sodomy is sometimes practiced between two men who alternately act as active and passive agents. Prof. Bhooshana Rao in his study has shown that in India, there is a class of male prostitutes commonly called "Eunuchs", whose main means of

living is by passive pederasty. They dress like women, and dress their hair in women fashion, wear ornaments, and adopt most tastes and habits of the females. He further pointed out that among these sexual inverts there are two distinct groups—*Hijirahs* and *Zenana*. The former group is deprived of their genitalia mostly before puberty, while the latter have them intact. The two groups live separately and preserve a line of demarcation between themselves and the female prostitutes.'

105. Only one citation of Hon'ble High Court of Madhya Pradesh could be made available on this subject i.e. **Prabhulal Vs. Raj Kunwarbai 1996 JLJ 151** wherein Hon'ble Justice N.K. Jain has laid down as under that "marriage of a man with another man or with a eunuch who is only a castrated man is void *abinitio*, such man or eunuch is not wife".

106. During the course of study of the subject, the case diary of Police Station Katni in reference of Crime no. 496/96 Section 302 IPC and the postmortem report of deceased Vishnu Gotia appended therein were also perused. As per the investigation report of Addl. S.P. annexed in the diary, it was found after the investigation of Crime no. 62/96 that deceased Vishnu Gotia was a eunuch. According to the postmortem report, his gonads were not found. Statements of deceased's wife, brother, sister etc. are also attached with the diary wherein all of them described him as male. In the postmortem report also, he has been referred as 40 year male.

107. In the book *"Hijadon Ka Sansar"* written by Shri Govind Singh and published by Anupam Books, Delhi in 1982 also, word eunuch has been defined like this that eunuch is the person who is without male gonads. According to the book, two eunuchs contested the elections in 1992 and they were classified in female category. In the election of 1977, a eunuch named Anarkali was fielded against George Fernandis and she was too categorized to as female but the stand was

changed thereafter. At the time of census of 1980, Government of India issued directions to categorize eunuchs in "Category-III", it was changed subsequently. In the directives issued for census in 1991 and 2001, the eunuchs were directed to be counted as male. Deputy Director Anand Kumar of the Office of the Registrar General, India, Ministry of Home Affairs, Government of India had also directed Ms. Sumita Ayub in the letter dated 02.01.1996 to keep accounts of eunuchs in the census as males. In the standing directions, Government has left the entry of sex of eunuchs at their will.

108. In addition to the above, I have made attempt to study the subject and the literature available in several magazines. From the gist of my entire study, the only thing which is inferred is that eunuch is a male who is castrated and deprived of potency.

109. In this regard, it is clear from the perusal of evidence available on record pertaining to respondent no.1 that his name stands recorded as male in the voter list of 1994 and 1999 of Assembly elections. In the voter list of 1994, name and parenthood were subsequently amended due to creeping of mistake but still the male gender was not amended which means that the fact of being a male is admitted. He being the male, Voter ID card No. 402105 was issued to him in 1995. Kamala @ Kamaluddin, respondent no.1 never attempted to get it amended nor raised any objection in the last 7 years against this. He opened the bank account in the name of Kamala @ Kamaluddin and even operated it. After acquiring house by way of succession from *guru* Nihora, all the mutation proceedings were executed in the form of male (eunuch). Even if entries in the voter list are taken to be recorded against the will under the Government directions even then the other documents (bank account and mutation register) prepared voluntarily are strong evidence of his being a male person. In this regard, the citation of **Ramji Dayawala**

**and Sons (P) Ltd. Vs. Invest Import AIR 1981, SC 2085** is worth perusing.

110. There is a clear evidence of the fact that respondent has been living right from the beginning in House no. 124 situated in Subhash ward. The house does not stand recorded in the name of Kamala parenthood "woman" but as per traditions, he has got it in succession from eunuch *guru* Nihora. On this house, is written name of Kamala @ Kamaluddin. Entire evidence in the former para and in this para remains non rebutted despite detailed cross-examination. Therefore, it is clear that respondent no. 1 is a male eunuch.

111. Respondent no.1 has described self as "female". He has stated about his birth as a female and claimed that she is a female. It is clear from the evidence adduced from and on his behalf that he has fabricated a story to prove this beyond the pleadings. In order to prove this, Tara Bai and Angoori Bai were produced as witnesses in the court and according to their version; they got respondent no. 1 as an orphan female child in Banda. They brought her up. She came to Katni at the age of 15-16 years. They emphatically stated that respondent no. 1 is a female by birth. The respondent Kamala Bai herself stated in the first line of the statement that she is a female and not a male or eunuch. PW K.L. Pandey has described her as a female on the basis of shape of breast and DW Abdul Kuddus and Ghasiram have stated her woman on the basis of her appearance in the dress up of a woman. The respondent has invited my attention towards the fact that as per the directions issued for the census of 2001, the eunuchs were given liberty to write their gender as per will.

112. It becomes clear from the appreciation of entire evidence that statements of Tara Bai and Angoori Bai very much suffer from infirmities and are contradictory. A statement of K.L. Pandey on this fact is unnatural being against the pleadings of the respondents and

against the affidavit filed before the Returning Officer. The respondent himself has not supported the alleged facts stated by Abdul Kuddus and Ghasiram. All these have been examined in detail while determining as to whether the respondent no.1 Kamala is having unknown parenthood or known parenthood and its repetition is not necessary.

113. The respondent has described herself as woman. The meaning of word woman in Oxford Dictionary is female sex. The meaning of female sex in the same dictionary is—"who is capable of producing ovum, or can produce offspring". There is no evidence showing that the respondent has got such capabilities.

114. It becomes clear from the study of this subject from the aspect of modern medical science (embryology) that eunuchs or hermaphrodite are of two types—one is the true and other one is pseudo. The true eunuchs or hermaphrodite are of two types–feminine and masculine. Similarly, true and pseudo ones are of two types–progesterone and estrogen. In a healthy male, total 23 pairs of chromosomes are found out of which 22 pairs are ordinary and one is the sex determining pair. Deformity in this produces eunuchs. It means that according to embryology, eunuchs may be male and female both but its identification may be ascertained from chromosomal analysis or DNA test.

115. In the *Bionature* Journal of 1998, it has been dealt in detail about eunuchs in the research article "Psychological Variables of Eunuchs-I Personality" by Sumita Ayub and Ayub Khan, which is reproduced as under—"various socio-anthropological studies say that all the eunuchs are not castrated ones, rather they include some congenital impotents (consisting of hermaphrodites and structurally as well as genetically deformed persons) and some true transvestites. Thus all the social scientists broadly classified eunuchs in the following categories: (i) *Qudarati Hijras,* (ii) *Hijras,* and (iii) *Zenanas.*

*Qudarati Hijras or congenital eunuchs:* They are born eunuchs and are of two types—

(a) Those who are born impotent. The born impotency may occur due to Congenital Testicular Deficiency or due to abnormal shape of the genital organs.

(b) Those who are hermaphrodites. According to Money (1969) biologically the sex of a baby is normally determined by fertilization of the X chromosome from the mother by either an X or Y bearing chromosome from the father.

Any error in the normal combination of sex chromosomes, i.e. (XX) for female and (XY) for male child may or may not affect an individual directly. *Klinefelters Syndrome* (XXY), morphologically a male child is born with rudimentary or defective male sex organs but the secondary female sexual characteristics grow at puberty. Similarly, such a wrong combination of sex chromosomes like the *Turner Syndrome* (XO) leaves unfinished external sexual differentiation of a baby.

*Hijras:* Castrated men are called *hijras,* whether they are impotent males or normal individuals. Salunke (1964) reported in his studies that 30 per cent eunuchs were costrated and rest was impotent. According to Vyas and Shingala (1987) 55 eunuchs were born eunuchs and 45 eunuchs acquired sexual deformity after birth out of the 100 eunuchs of Baroda City.

*Zenanas:* They are normal men having their families but due to the pecuniary condition or for their psychological satisfaction they put on female attire and join the eunuch community. In true sense, they are transvestites. Whatever be the types of eunuchs the whole community share the same traditions, customs and rituals concerning—(i) Birth or initiation of eunuchs, (ii) Professional life, and (iii) Death...."

116. Again the problem here is that this fact can be determined only from the intensive medical investigations.

117. Here one important fact is worth mentioning that petitioners had prayed for medical examination of the

respondent. A separate application in this regard was filed at the preliminary stage of the petition and even during the final hearing of the petition, an application was filed but it was vehemently opposed by the respondent at all occasions with the support of written statements. Looking at the legal and constitutional aspects, the Hon'ble Court rejected the final petition of the respondents on 26.07.2002.But it has left many questions unanswered. In such conditions theories are propounded against the outlooks of judicial illustrations viz. **Bipinchandra Shantilal Bhatt Vs. Madhuriben Bhatt AIR 1963 Gujarat 250, Probhat Kumar Mitra Vs. Sukriti Mitra AIR 1971 Calcutta 1, Maragathamani Vs. Ebenezer Ponraj Samuel AIR 1971 Madras 27, Venkatanarayan Vs. Kurupati Laxmi Devi AIR 1985 AP 1**. In this way, in the present case the petitions not only lack medical and scientific evidences, but also it strengthens the theory of probability which leads to the fact that the respondent no. 1 is a male.

118. Therefore, it is clear from the aforesaid discussion that from the perspective of religious, historical, linguistic and etymological angles that from time immemorial; the eunuchs have always been regarded as males as per the information secured and they have been addressed too accordingly. Today, medical science, though has stated two genders male and female of eunuchs, but this does not put them as being against the concept of females because as per Section 10 of the IPC and the dictionary meanings as discussed above, the "woman" is defined as "female sex" and the word "female sex" is defined as "one who produces ovum or offspring". According to medical science, any eunuch may be a female eunuch but he cannot be regarded as a "female" looking to meaning of woman.

119. In addition to the above, when we specifically study the evidence regarding the respondent, we find that he is neither a born female because the evidence leads

to show that he does not know about the natural morphological structure of a woman and never had any desire for sexual intercourse nor is there any evidence which could show that he is a female eunuch. Thus, there is no question regarding him, a "female".

120. Therefore, from the foregone discussion, following is the quintessence of the findings—
    1. Respondent no. 1 is Kamala s/o Nihora and not Kamala s/o unknown.
    2. He is a eunuch.
    3. Eunuchs are generally castrated males.
    4. Respondent no. 1 is also a male eunuch.
    5. Respondent no. 1 is not a "female".

121. Consequently, it may be inferred that respondent no.1 was not eligible to contest election from the seat reserved for females of general category. Acceptance of nomination form by the Returning Officer was improper and his election in the suit election is illegal.

### *Issue no. 5*

122. Petitioner Kamendra Singh and respondent no. 3 have prayed for a relief that in the event of declaration of the election of respondent no.1 as void, the respondent no. 3 may be declared returned. Petitioner Namita Chauhan has prayed to declare the election as void and for conducting fresh poll and some parties have prayed to declare returned the respondent no. 2 Aradhana Jain, a candidate of Congress Party. The parties have submitted detailed arguments in this regard.

123. The petitioner and respondent no. 3 have stated that voters were misled due to wrong nomination of respondent no. 1. Had the nomination form of the respondent no.1 not been accepted, all the votes secured by him would have been cast in favour of the respondent no. 3. They have also argued that if the total votes secured by respondent no.1 are not taken into

account, she would be declared elected by virtue of securing second highest votes in the election.

124. Respondent no. 2 has argued that along with the suit election, election to the post of Councillor was also held on party basis. It is clear from the computation of the total votes that the Congress supported candidates secured the maximum votes. Had respondent no.1 not been fielded in the array, all his votes would have been cast in favour of respondent no. 2. The respondent no.1 has supported this. Other petitioners and respondents have opposed. The parties have produced judicial citations in this regard viz. **AIR 1969 SC 604 Vishwanatha Reddy Vs. Konappa Rudrappa Nadgouda and others; (2002) 5 SCC 568 Prakash Khandre Vs. Dr. Vijay Kumar Khandre and others; AIR 1993 SC 95 D.K. Sharma Vs. Ram Sharan Yadav and others.**

125. In the citation adduced by the petitioner **(AIR 1969 SC 604)**, Hon'ble Court has laid down that if some votes were obtained by the returned candidate by corrupt practices, the court is bound to declare the petitioner or another candidate elected, on the condition that the votes obtained by the returned candidate by corrupt practice, such candidate would have obtained a majority of votes. The votes obtained by corrupt practice by the returned candidate, proved to be guilty of corrupt practice, are expressly excluded in the computation of total votes for ascertaining whether a majority of votes had been obtained by the defeated candidate and no fresh poll is necessary.

126. In the case cited by the petitioner, there were only two candidates in the array of election and the disqualified candidate was facing the allegations of corrupt practice. The facts of the present case are different and, therefore, the said citation has no application in this case.

127. Considering the citation **AIR 1993 SC 95** cited by the petitioner and the respondent himself, Hon'ble

Supreme Court of India laid down in **(2002)5 SCC 568** that where more than two candidates are contesting the election for one post and subsequently the returned candidate is found disqualified, the candidate securing the maximum votes amongst the remaining candidates, cannot be declared elected. Under such circumstances, the votes cast in favour of the disqualified candidate can neither be treated as thrown away nor a presumption can be drawn that such votes would have been cast in the favour of the second highest vote catcher. It cannot be predicted as to in whose favour the voters would have cast their votes if they are aware of the fact that the returned candidate is disqualified.

128. The arguments advanced by the other parties regarding the poll are merely probabilities and no judgment can be based on conjectures and possibilities. The citation produced by the Petitioner Kamendra Singh has no application in the present case due to difference in facts because in the light of judgment by the Apex Court, the result cannot be computed excluding the votes obtained by the respondent no.1. Under such circumstances, I do not deem it proper to declare any other candidate elected in place of respondent no.1. Therefore, this issue is determined in negation.

***Issue no. 8***

129. The respondent has also raised the objection that no objection was raised against the voter list. An appeal could have been preferred against the wrong entry thereof. This was not done by the petitioner and, therefore, the entry cannot be challenged now. But in the present petition, voter list is not challenged but the election itself. It has already been decided that such a challenge is valid. Therefore, the objection of the respondent is not liable to be sustained.

130. It has also been prayed to dismiss the petition for non-joinder of Returning Office but he was impleaded in

Election Petition No. 14/2000 which was afterwards deleted as unnecessary vide order dated 13.11.2000. No action has since been taken against that order; therefore, the same cannot be questioned again.

131. Having regard to the foregone discussion, I reach to a conclusion that the petitioners succeeded in proving that—
   1. Respondent no. 1 is Kamala S/o Nihora and not Kamala s/o unknown.
   2. He is a eunuch.
   3. Eunuchs are generally castrated males.
   4. Respondent no. 1 is also a male eunuch.
   5. Respondent no. 1 is not a "female".

132. But in the present case, the circumstances do not appear to exist that in place of respondent no. 1, the second highest vote catcher, respondent no. 3 or any other respondent could be considered proper as elected, therefore, the prayer of the petitioners and other respondents is disallowed.

133. As a result, all the petitions filed by the petitioners are allowed.

134. The election of respondent no. 1 for the post of Mayor in the election of Municipal Corporation, Katni held in December, 1999 is declared void.

135. Respondent no. 1 and petitioners shall bear their own cost.

136. Counsel fee be included in the cost as per certificate if certified or the as per the table, whichever is less.

Judgment pronounced in the open court.
Typed at my dictation.

*Sd/-*

*(Virender Singh)*
*I Addl. District Judge*
*Katni*

# Bibliography


Ali, Mrs. M. Hasan, (1974), *Observations on the Mussalmans of India.* Edited with notes and an introduction by W. Crooke, 1917. Reprint. Karachi: Oxford University Press.

Anderson, Mary M., (1990), *Hidden Power: The Palace Eunuchs of Imperical China.* New York: Prometheus Books.

Atal, Yogesh, (1971), *Local Communities and National Politics.* Delhi: National Publishing House.

Ayalon, D., (1977), The Eunuchs in the Mamluk Sultanate. *In* Myrium Rosen-Ayalon (ed.), *Studies in Memory of Gaston Wiet.* Jerusalem: Institute of Asian and African Studies, The Hebrew University of Jerusalem.

Ayub, Sumita and Khan, Ayub, (1998), Self-concept in Eunuchs. *Eastern Anthropologist,* 55(4), 25–30.

Bakshi, Sandeep, (2004), A Comparative Analysis of Hijras and Drag Queens: The Subversive Possibilities and Limits of Parading Effeminacy and Negotiating Masculinity. *Journal of Homosexuality,* 40 (3-4), 211-223.

Barnett, Richard B., (1987), *North India between Empires: Awadh, the Mughals and the British 1720-1801.* Delhi: Manohar.

Bhatt, Ravi, (2006), *The Life and Times of the Nawabs of Lucknow.* N. Delhi: Rupa & Co.

Butler, David, (1958), *The Study of Political Behaviour.* London: Hutchinson University.

Chatterjee, Indrani, (1999), *Gender, Slavery and Law in Colonial India.* New Delhi: Oxford University Press.

Cohen, Lawrence, (1995), The Pleasures of Castration: The postoperative status of hijras, jankhas and academics *In* Paul R. Abramson and Steven D. Pinkerton (Eds.), *Sexual Nature, Sexual Culture* (pp. 276-304). Chicago: University of Chicago Press.

Coser, Lewis A., (1964), The Political Functions of Eunuchism. *American Sociological Review,* 29 (1-6), 880-885.

Dalrymple, William, (1992), *City of Djinns.* Delhi: Indus.

Donzel, E., Lewis, B. and Pellat, Ch., (1978), *Encyclopaedia of Islam,* Vol. IV. Leiden: E.J. Brill.

Durkheim, Emile, (1950), *The Rules of Sociological Method,* Glencoe, III: The Free Press.

Eberhard, W., (1960), *A History of China.* Berkeley and Los Angeles: University of California Press.

*Encyclopaedia of Religion and Ethics,* (1981), James Hastings (ed.) Vol. V. New York: Charles Scribner's Sons.

Faridi, F.L., (1899), Hijdas *In* J.M. Campbell (Compiler). *Gazetteer of the Bombay Presidency* (Vol.9, pt. 2:21-22) *Gujarat Population, Musalmans and Parsis.* Bombay: Government Central Press.

Habib, M. and Nizami, K.A. (Eds.), (1970), *A Comprehensive History of India,* Vol. V, The Delhi Sultanate (A.D. 1206-1526). Published under the auspices of The Indian History Congress. New Delhi: People's Publishing House.

Hall, Kira, (1997), "Go Suck Your Husband's Sugarcane!" Hijras and the Use of Sexual Insult. *In* Anna Livia and Kira Hall (Eds.), *Queerly Phrased: Language, Gender and Sexuality.* New York: Oxford University Press.

Hambly, Gavin, (1974), A note on the trade in eunuchs in Mughal Bengal. *Journal of American Oriental Society,* 94(1), 125-130.

Jaros, Dean and Grant, Lawrence, V. (1974), *Political Behaviour.* Basil Blackwell: Oxford.

Khan, Ayub and Ayub, Sumita, (2002), Psychological Variables of Eunuchs-I (Personality). *Bionature,* 81(1), 351-357.

Kumar, P. (1964), *Personality Study of Student Leadership,* Unpublished Doctoral Thesis, Allahabad University, Allahabad (India).

Lal, K.S. (1988), *The Mughal Harem.* New Delhi: Aditya Prakashan.

Lazarsfeld, P.F., Bernard Berelson and Hazel Gaudet (1944), *The People's Choice.* New York: Columbia University Press.

Lockhart, Laurence, (1958), *The fall of the Safavi dynasty and the Afghan Occupation of Persia.* New York: Cambridge University Press.

Malik, Faris, (1999), Born Eunuchs: Homosexual Identity in the Ancient. World.<http://www.well.com/user/aquarius>.

Marmon, S., (1995), *Eunuchs and Sacred Boundaries in Islamic Society.* New York and Oxford: Oxford University Press.

Mcclosky, H., (1968), *Political Participation. In* David L. Sills and Robert K. Merton (eds.) *International Encyclopedia of the Social Sciences.* New York: MacMillan.

Mehta, S., (1947), Eunuchs, Pavaiyas and Hijadas. *In Gujarat Sahitya Sabha, Amdavad, Karyavahi* (pt. II, pp. 3-75). Ahmedabad, India.

Mills, C. Wright, (1956), *The Power Elite.* New York: Oxford University Press.

Mitamura, Taisuke, (1970), *Chinese Eunuchs: The Structure of Intimate Politics* (trans.) C.A. Pomeroy. Tokyo and Vermont: Charles Tuttle.

Nanda, Serena, (1990), *Neither Man nor Woman: The Hijras of India.* Belmont California: Wadsworth Publishing Company.

Nanda, Serena, (2002), Life on the Margins: A Hijra's Story. *In* Diane P. Mines and Sarah Lamb (Eds.) *Everyday Life in South Asia* (pp. 159-166). Bloomington: Indiana University Press.

Peterson, Steven A., (1990), *Political Behaviour.* California: Sage Publications.

Raghuvanshi, M. and Navalkar, P., (1980), The Third Sex. *Probe India,* November, pp. 10-19.

Ranade, S.N., (1983), *A Study of Eunuchs in Delhi.* Unpublished manuscript, University of Delhi, Delhi.

Rawlinson, George, (2001), *The Five Great Monarchies of the Ancient Eastern World,* (Paperback). Vol. III. Elibron Classics Series. London: Adamant Media Corporation.

Reddy, Gayatri, (2003), "Men" who would be kings: celibacy, emasculation, and the re-production of hijras in contemporary Indian politics—gender identity, social stigma, and political corruption. *Social Research,* 70(1), 163-200.

Russell, R.V. and Hiralal, R.B., (1916), *The Tribes and Castes of the Central Provinces of India* (Vol. III, pp. 206-212). London: McMillan and Co. Ltd.

Saeed, Mian Muhammad, (1972), *The Sharqi Sultanate of Jaunpur* (1394-1495). Karachi: University of Karachi, Pakistan.

Saletore, R.N., (1974), *Sex Life under Indian Rulers.* Delhi: Hind Pocket Books.

Salunke, G.R., (1976), The cult of the hijaras. *Illustrated Weekly of India,* August 8, pp. 16-21. Bombay: Times of India.

Sarkar, Jadunath, (1964), *Fall of the Mughal Empire* (III ed.), Vol. 1, Calcutta: M.C. Sarkar Sons.

Satyal, Amita, (2001), Hijras and the Politics of Empowerment in Contemporary India. *Harvard Asia Quarterly,* 5(3), Summer.

Shah, A.M., (1961), A note on the hijadas of Gujarat. *American Anthropologist,* 61, 1325-1330.

Sharma, S.K., (1984), Eunuchs: Past and Present. *Eastern Anthropologist,* 37(4), 381-389.

Sinha, A.P., (1967), Procreation among the Eunuchs. *Eastern Anthropologist*, 21(2), 168-176.

Sirsikar, V.M., (1965), *Political Behaviour in India*. Bombay: Manaktalas.

Thurston, E. and Rangachari, K., (1909), *Castes and Tribes of Southern India* (Vol. III, pp. 288-292). Madras: Government Press.

Toledono, E.R., (1984), The Imperial Eunuchs of Istanbul: From Africa to the Heart of Islam. *Middle Eastern Studies*, 20(3): 379-390.

Van Buitenen, J.A.B., (1984), *Mahabharata*. Vol. 3. The Book of Virata. Chicago: University of Chicago Press.

Verba, S. and Nie, N.H., (1972), *Participation in America*. New York: Harper & Row.

Verba, S., Nie, N.H. and Kim, Jae-On, (1978), *Participation and Political Equality*. Cambridge: Cambridge University Press.

Verma, S.P. and Narain, Iqbal *et al.*, (1973), *Voting Behaviour in a Changing Society*. Meerut: Meenakshi Prakashan.

Vinayak, Ramesh, (1998), Out of the Shadows. *India Today*, March 21, p. 10.

Vyas, M.D. and Shingala, Y., (1987), *The Life Style of the Eunuchs*. New Delhi: Anmol Publications.

Weber, Max, (1951), *The Religion of China* (trans. and ed.) Hans Gerth. Glencoe, Ill: The Free Press.

Wittfogel, Karl August, (1963), *Oriental Despotism*. New Haven: Yale University Press.

# Index